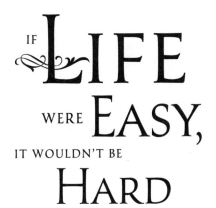

IF **LIFE** WERE **EASY,**
IT WOULDN'T BE
HARD

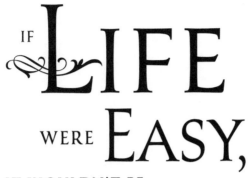

IF LIFE WERE EASY, IT WOULDN'T BE HARD

and Other Reassuring Truths

SHERI DEW

**DESERET
BOOK**

SALT LAKE CITY, UTAH

Photo on page 76 taken by Jay Ward

Library of Congress Cataloging-in-Publication Data

Dew, Sheri L.
    If life were easy, it wouldn't be hard : and other reassuring truths / Sheri Dew.
        p.   cm.
    Includes index.
    ISBN 1-59038-538-1 (hardbound : alk. paper)
 1. Christian life—Mormon authors.   I. Title.
    BX8656.D47   2005
    248.4'893—dc22   2005023000

Printed in the United States of America   72076
Publishers Printing, Salt Lake City, UT

10   9   8   7   6   5   4   3   2   1

To a dear friend,
whose prodding and encouragement
willed this into being

CONTENTS

Chapter One

IF LIFE WERE EASY, IT WOULDN'T BE HARD

A few months ago, I had an assignment that required me to make a quick, long-weekend-type trip to Nauvoo, and it seemed like the perfect opportunity to take a nephew and two nieces with me. My nephew had just received his mission call, one niece was preparing to turn in her mission papers, and the other niece was getting ready to graduate from high school. Realizing that all of their lives were soon to change, I couldn't help but seize the chance to spend a long weekend with these three spectacular young adults I love in a place I love.

We gathered at the Salt Lake City airport for a Friday evening flight to St. Louis, from where we would drive the remaining two and a half hours to Nauvoo. We knew we wouldn't get to Nauvoo until late, but there was nothing pressing early the next morning, so no problem. We arrived at the airport, checked in, and boarded the aircraft. A few minutes later, the plane took off and headed east toward Missouri.

The flight attendant had served refreshments to about half of the passengers on the relatively small plane when the captain interrupted our reverie with the kind of announcement you never like to hear coming from a cockpit when that cockpit is at 35,000 feet: "Ladies and gentlemen, I'm sorry to tell you we've got some good news and some bad news." He paused, then went on: "The bad news is that we just lost a hydraulic 'something-or-other.' The good news is that we've got a backup onboard and it appears to be working. Ground control advises us, however, that we must return to Salt Lake City. So we're turning back west."

The passengers groaned audibly, and the flight attendant began gathering up everything she'd just handed out. Then, we waited. And waited. And waited. We had been in flight about thirty minutes, which suggested it would take about that long to return to Salt Lake City. But after a much longer period of time had passed, and the tension among the passengers onboard the crippled airliner was starting to be palpable, the captain finally put us out of our misery with another announcement: "Ladies and gentlemen, I apologize for the delay, but I've got only good news this time. Our mechanics now tell us that because the backup part seems to be functioning fine, we can resume our trip to St. Louis. So we are turning back east."

Once again, the flight attendant brought out the refreshment cart and began to make her way down the aisle. She had just about had time to serve everyone when the pilot broke the silence again: "Ladies and gentlemen, this is most embarrassing, but our mechanics are now telling us they feel uneasy about the backup part functioning properly all the way to St. Louis, and we have again been advised to return to Salt Lake City."

This time there were moans and groans all around. We finally landed *back* in Salt Lake City at almost precisely the same time we should have been landing in St. Louis. We'd been traveling nearly three hours and were right back where we started! By the time we set foot back inside the airport and were told we'd have to wait for a replacement plane to be brought to our gate, I had *completely* lost all enthusiasm for going to Nauvoo. So I turned to my nieces and nephew and asked if we shouldn't just bag the trip and spend the weekend at my house. To which my nephew instantly replied, "Are you kidding? This is an adventure!" I felt compelled to point out the obvious, that at the rate we were going, by the time we finally did get to Nauvoo it would be the middle of the night, if not the following morning. That was when one of my nieces interrupted with this piece of wisdom: "And besides, Aunt Sheri, don't you know? If life were easy, it wouldn't be hard."

What she said made me laugh right out loud. But then I began to think about how profound her comment was.

It's true that if life were easy, it wouldn't be hard. Meaning this: What if every prayer were instantly answered in the way we wanted it to be? What if a little bit of spiritual due diligence now and again kept us in constant and clear contact with our Heavenly Father? If nothing ever tested our faith or our resolve or our convictions—because we really don't know what we believe or believe *in*, for that matter, until we're tested—then what are the chances we would progress far enough spiritually in this lone and dreary world? Whether we like it or not, our trials and struggles can tend to accelerate our push toward godliness. In fact, it's possible we wouldn't go as far as we're capable of going without them. "For all those who will not endure chastening . . . cannot be sanctified" (D&C 101:5).

Brigham Young said that "God never bestows upon His people, or upon an individual, superior blessings without a severe trial to prove them" (*Journal of Discourses*, 3:206). Sounds a bit foreboding on the one hand. But on the other, surely we couldn't expect to inherit the gift of eternal life or to receive ongoing bestowals of charity or to be taught the mysteries of godliness or to learn to communicate clearly with the heavens without making a diligent, consistent effort—in other words, without it requiring a lot of spiritual work.

A friend of mine has sometimes wondered out loud what the headline in the *Rocky Ridge Gazette* might have been if those who pushed, pulled, and prayed their handcarts over that forbidding Wyoming terrain hadn't kept going: "Turned Back Because of Rain." Or, "Turned Back for Fatigue." Or, "Turned Back Because It Was Too Hard."

This life was designed to be a test—a test to determine if we want to be part of the kingdom of God more than we want anything else.

They didn't turn back. And neither can we.

This life was designed to be a test—a test to determine if we want to be part of the kingdom of God more than we want anything else. Mortality offers a wide range of experiences and opportunities, everything from countless ways to serve our fellowman to an endless array of distractions, deceptions, and modes of self-gratification. When all is said and done, perhaps the most fundamental question we each answer is, Do we want to be part of the kingdom of God—both here on earth and eternally—more than we want anything else? And do we demonstrate by our choices and priorities, by how we live our lives—everything from the way we spend our time and energy to the way we spend our influence and resources—what we really care about?

After being expelled from the Garden, Eve capsulized the mortal experience in this spiritually powerful, single-sentence sermon: "Were it not for our transgression we never should have had seed, and never should have known good and evil, and the joy of our redemption, and the eternal life which God giveth unto all the obedient" (Moses 5:11). In short, during our mortal sojourn we can expect to experience joy and pain and everything in between.

Said the Prophet Joseph, "A religion that does not require the sacrifice of all things never has power sufficient to produce the faith necessary unto life and salvation" (*Lectures on Faith*, 6:7). As the Book of Mormon prophet Amaleki admonished his brethren, it is for us to determine if we will "offer [our] whole souls as an offering unto [the Lord] (Omni 1:26). If we do, and if we "seek the riches which it is the will of the Father to give unto [us], [we] shall be the richest of all people, for [we] shall have the riches of eternity" (D&C 38:39). For "the Lord is merciful unto *all* who will, in the sincerity of their hearts, call upon his holy name. . . . The gate of heaven is open unto *all*, even to those who will believe on the name of Jesus Christ, who is the Son of God" (Helaman 3:27–28; emphasis added).

I've had an aversion to addressing the subject of life's difficulty—which is frighteningly close to the topic of "enduring to the end"—for as long as I can remember, not because I don't want to endure to the end or don't intend to endure to the end, but because enduring-to-the-end messages usually make life seem hard and dreary and like a sentence to the proverbial life on the rock pile. But, in reality, life is supposed to be a test, albeit an open-book test, considering the countless resources we may turn to on a constant basis.

Our mortal experience is designed to test what we really care about, what we really believe, what we really want to become, and how we really feel about our Father and His Son. Imagine if during the premortal council in heaven, when our Father laid out His plan for us, He had said, "Please listen, I need to know if you care about me and my Son, your Elder Brother, and His gospel. And I need to know if you really want to follow the plan, so I'm going to send you down to earth where you can make choices while being separated from us. But don't worry, if it gets very hard, I'll ease it up." It wouldn't be much of a test, would it? It's more likely that He said something like, "When things get difficult, whatever *you* do, don't ease up—don't ease up on your efforts to seek after me, to communicate with me, to learn about me. Because that is what will get you through." For "this life is the time for men to prepare to meet God" (Alma 34:32), and surely no one would expect to meet Him—in this life or the next—without having worked diligently to overcome weaknesses and, through faith, to become "perfect in Christ" (Moroni 10:32).

We don't really know what we believe in or care about until what we believe in or care about is threatened, challenged, or measured.

We don't really know what we believe in or care about until what we believe in or care about is threatened, challenged, or measured. We don't really know if we care about being virtuous men and women until our virtue is tested by some glaring temptation right in front of us. We don't really find out if we are men and women of integrity until unobserved opportunities to compromise our integrity present themselves. We don't know if we'll stand up for what we believe until we must do so in a hostile or at least skeptical environment.

Nearly ten years ago my brother, two years younger than I, died suddenly of a heart attack. Not only could I not remember life without Steve—my very earliest memory is of waking up to find Grandma tending me because Mother was at the hospital delivering her second child—but he was a trusted confidant, someone who could always make me laugh and whom I counted on to remain cool, calm, and collected in any situation. When Steve died, it felt like a piece of me died.

As I stood by his casket for the last time, I had two clear reactions: First, I'd never been so happy to see anyone dressed in temple clothing, and second, I remember thinking to myself, "Okay, Sheri, do you believe it, or don't you? Do you believe in eternal life? Do you believe you'll see your brother again? Do you believe that he is sealed to his wife and his children, and that he will always be your brother? Or don't you?"

It was a sweet and affirming moment. Even as the questions ran across my mind, I knew that, yes, I did believe all those beautiful, reassuring doctrines, and more. And amidst the tugging, aching emotions of the moment, I also felt a surge of confidence and peace.

Not long ago I visited with a marvelous group of young adults in Aarau, Switzerland. At the beginning of our conversation, I asked them to tell me what was hard about being a young adult member of the Church in Switzerland. Their answers were astute and comprehensive and, in many respects, similar to responses young adults in many other parts of the world have given. Toward the end of the conversation, however, one young man's comment seemed to encapsulate all the others. "I've been home from my mission a few months," he began. "I loved my mission and worked as hard as I could. I thought that when I got home, I would find someone to marry, get an education, and start a career. But," and then he paused, searching for the words, finally concluding, "I thought it would be easier than it is to find my way."

I didn't have the heart to tell him that he's just at the front end of the process of finding his way—a process that can at times be scary, intimidating, confusing, puzzling, and downright gut-wrenching. For all of the challenges and worries President Gordon B. Hinckley has faced during his ninety-five years of living, it is possible that he would say the death of his beloved wife, Marjorie, has presented him with the most grueling challenge of his life. He has been candid about his feelings. Speaking at the funeral of Elder Neal A. Maxwell little more than three months after the passing of Sister Hinckley, he said, directing these comments specifically to Sister Maxwell: "As one who has recently passed through this ordeal, I think I know something of what lies ahead of you. At funerals we speak words intended to give comfort. But in reality they afford but little comfort. Only those who have passed through this dark valley know of its utter desolation. To lose one's much-loved partner with whom one has long walked through sunshine and shadow is absolutely devastating."

And yet, we once again see in President Hinckley's life an example to follow. Despite suffering such a ravaging loss at an age when many would simply give up, and with the weight of the Church and indeed the world on his shoulders, he keeps marching on.

Other prophets have done likewise. The Nephite civilization had crumbled when Moroni wrote poignantly: "I had supposed not to have written more, but I have not as yet perished; and I make not myself known to the Lamanites lest they should destroy me. For behold . . . they put to death every Nephite that will not deny the Christ. And I, Moroni, will not deny the Christ; wherefore, I wander whithersoever I can for the safety of mine own life" (Moroni 1:1–3). It's hard to contemplate the suffocating sense of loneliness Moroni must have felt. His father had been killed. His friends were gone. The Lamanites were hunting him. He couldn't believe he was still alive. But he was, and though he hadn't expected to write more, what he subsequently recorded prior to his death was remarkable: sacrament prayers, discourses on the Spirit of Christ and the conversion and activation of members, clarifications regarding infant baptism and the decline of the Nephite civilization, and the most classic discourse on faith, hope, and charity in all of scripture. In the face of undeniable loneliness and heartache, Moroni didn't give up either. He kept going until the end.

Likewise, there have been literally millions of men and women in this dispensation who have carried on when it would have been easier to just give up. There is a headstone in the Old Nauvoo Cemetery at the head of Parley Street that marks the graves of infant twins born to the Scovils. Lucius Scovil, who ran one of Nauvoo's bakeries, had lost everything when he was driven from Missouri. He arrived in Illinois penniless, only to have his family stricken with fever and malaria. He worshiped and suffered with the Saints in Nauvoo, and about the time of the trek west, his wife died giving birth to the twins. Ten days later the twins died also.

After a time, Lucius prepared to go west with the Saints, but while making final preparations, he received a mission call to England. He traveled with his surviving family members a few days west into the prairie to help them get started and to make arrangements for someone to care for them. He blessed them and then, leaving them collapsed in tears, turned back east to head for a mission six thousand miles away without purse or scrip.

He wrote, simply: "This seemed like a painful duty for me to perform, to leave my family to go into the wilderness and I to turn and go the other way. It cost all that I had on this earth, . . . [but] I thought it was best to round up my shoulders like a bold soldier . . . and assist in rolling forth the Kingdom of God" (Maurine Jensen Proctor and Scot Facer Proctor, *The Gathering*, 92).

Bathsheba Smith, who would serve as the fourth general president of the Relief Society, wrote this about leaving Nauvoo: "We left a comfortable home, the accumulations of four years of labor and thrift and took away with us only a few much needed articles such as clothing, bedding, and provisions. We left everything else behind us for our enemies. My last act in that precious spot was to tidy the rooms, sweep up the floor, and set the broom in its accustomed place behind the door. Then with emotions in my heart which I could not now pen and which I then strove with success to conceal, I gently closed the door and faced an unknown future, faced a new life, a greater destiny as I well knew, but I faced it with faith in God. . . . I was going into the wilderness, but I was going with the man I loved dearer than my life. I had my little children. I had heard a voice, so I stepped into the wagon with a certain degree of serenity" (Carol Cornwall Madsen, *In Their Own Words: Women and the Story of Nauvoo*, 213).

How did she do it? How did Lucius Scovil and Moroni do it? How is President Hinckley doing it? And how do we keep going even when circumstances or events seem to sap the last ounce of our physical, emotional, or spiritual energy? How do we keep going, considering the fact that we are undergoing our test in what prophets, seers, and revelators have indicated is the most grueling, intense period in the history of the earth?

Said President Boyd K. Packer at a J. Reuben Clark Law Society devotional, "These are days of great spiritual danger. . . . The world is spiraling downward at an ever-quickening pace. I am sorry to tell you that it will not get better. I know of nothing in the history of the Church or in the history of the world to compare with our present circumstances. Nothing happened in Sodom and Gomorrah which exceeds the wickedness and depravity which surrounds us now" ("On the Shoulders of Giants," 28 February 2004).

To make matters worse, the blatant evil of ancient Sodom and Gomorrah was not instantly broadcast by satellite around the world and around the clock, as it is today. The cumulative effect of this barrage of evil carried through every imaginable form of media is devastating. Evil breeds evil. And constant exposure to evil that even a few years ago would have horrified *any* God-fearing man or woman, regardless of religious or cultural beliefs, spawns familiarity. Sexually explicit material, behaviors, and lifestyles that were talked about in hushed tones and found only in dark alleys when I was young are now embraced as liberating, open-minded, and, worst of all, as normal. Familiarity breeds normality, meaning it makes aberrant behavior seem and *feel* normal. And anytime Lucifer convinces a man or woman—or, most horrifying, a society—that unrighteous behavior is normal, he has made inroads that are difficult to combat and almost impossible to reverse.

So again, how can we ensure that though life is meant to be rigorous, we do what we have come here to do and live up to who we are as latter-day men and women of God?

There is only one answer: by living the gospel of Jesus Christ. And that is possible *only* if we obtain a personal witness of Jesus Christ and Him crucified.

The prophet Mormon provides a stirring example for our day. The description of the era in which he was born and raised is sobering. Wickedness prevailed upon the face of the land to such an extreme that the Lord had removed His disciples. The work of miracles and healing had ceased because of the iniquity of the people, the Holy Ghost was not being given to anyone, and sorceries and witchcrafts had invaded the land such that "the power of the evil one was wrought upon all the face of the land" (see Mormon 1:13, 14, 19). Mormon recorded that "there never had been so great wickedness among all the children of Lehi" (Mormon 4:12).

And yet, not only did Mormon live a spectacularly

faithful life, but he raised (presumably with his wife) a spectacularly faithful prophet-son, Moroni. How did he do it?

The key seems to be in one verse, in which he related the following: "And I, being fifteen years of age and being somewhat of a sober mind, therefore I was visited of the Lord, and tasted and knew of the goodness of Jesus" (Mormon 1:15).

It is not clear from that scripture what being "visited of the Lord" means. Mormon may have had a vision or dream. He may have experienced an overpowering witness of the Spirit. But whatever the nature of his experience, it seems to have shaped his destiny. At a young age he began to learn for himself of the divinity and power of Jesus Christ. He tasted and knew of the goodness, the pure love, of Jesus Christ. Surely this experience charted his course for the remainder of his life.

The same is true for each of us. When we obtain for ourselves a witness that Jesus is the Christ, that His gospel has been restored to the earth, that His prophet leads and guides His Church, and that all of the power and ordinances necessary to purify, sanctify, and exalt us are on the earth today, there can be no turning back.

Further, as our understanding of what the Father has promised us and what the Savior did for us increases, our love for them increases so much that we're willing to do whatever they ask us to do. Imagine: *All* that the Father has is potentially ours. All! Nothing held back. We have the potential of being joint-heirs with Christ. It's difficult not to wonder—at least when seeing it through a mortal lens—how such an exquisite, ultimate reward can possibly be fair, considering what He did for us. Is it fair that He would take all the pains and sins and suffering of the world upon Him, yet we are eligible to be joint-heirs with Him? It seems almost too good to be true. Yet it is!

The Prophet Joseph and Sidney Rigdon learned in vision the major factor distinguishing those who will inherit the telestial and terrestrial kingdoms from those who stand to inherit celestial glory. Those assigned to the telestial kingdom "received not the gospel, neither the testimony of Jesus"; those relegated to the terrestrial kingdom "received not the testimony of Jesus in the flesh, but afterwards received it"; but those who inherit celestial glory "received the testimony of Jesus, and believed on his name and were baptized" (D&C 76:101, 74, 51).

How important is a testimony of Jesus Christ? It is everything!

Prophets testify of Christ. The scriptures testify of Christ. The Holy Ghost testifies of Christ. As we immerse ourselves in the words of prophets, seers, and revelators; as we immerse ourselves in the scriptures; and as we diligently seek to learn the language of revelation by learning to hear the voice of the Spirit, we place ourselves in a position to steadily increase our personal witness of the Savior and our determination to follow Him at all cost.

While we have been assigned to take the test of mortality during the most spiritually rigorous and demanding time in the world's history, we have not been left alone.

In short, if life were easy, we would have nothing to show for our time here. President Boyd K. Packer said: "Life will not be free from challenges, some of them bitter and hard to bear. We may wish to be spared all the trials of life, but that would be contrary to the great plan of happiness, 'for it must needs be, that there is an opposition in all things' (2 Nephi 2:11). This testing is the source of our strength" (*Ensign,* May 2004, 80).

While we have been assigned to take the test of mortality during the most spiritually rigorous and demanding time in the world's history, we have not been left alone. Most of the people who have ever lived in this world have faced their trials with no access to the fulness of the gospel of Jesus Christ.

But we have that gospel. We have the gift and the power of the Holy Ghost. We have the gift and the power of saving ordinances that bind us to each other and to the Lord. We have the power of the priesthood on the earth and the gift of full access to that power. We have the gift of a prophet, seer, and revelator who holds all the keys of the kingdom. We have the gift of revealed scripture and the power contained in the Word of God. And we have the gift of understanding that the Atonement of Jesus Christ is filled with both redemptive and enabling power.

All of which explains why the Lord would encourage us: "Be of good cheer, and do not fear, for I the Lord am with you, and will stand by you; and ye shall bear record of me, even Jesus Christ, that I am the Son of the living God, that I was, that I am, and that I am to come" (D&C 68:6).

I've seen what happens to men and women who embody this truth—meaning, whose lives and attitudes and even faces reflect the good cheer borne of testimony. My first trip to Africa was life-changing in this respect. From our first day there, my traveling companions and I commented on how happy the people were—particularly the women. We saw them walking alongside the road carrying bundles and burdens bigger than they were, and they were always smiling. Though the privation with which many of them dealt was obvious, they spoke readily about the joy of their lives: their testimonies of Jesus Christ.

An episode in Accra, Ghana, is unforgettable. I had asked a large group of women, all Church leaders, to help me understand the unique challenges they faced. They were slow to respond and seemed to struggle with the question. Finally a beautiful African woman raised her hand and said, "Sister Dew, we do have challenges here, but we believe in Jesus Christ, and so we are happy." And they *were* happy—perhaps the happiest group of women I've ever met or observed. As I flew back to the United States, I couldn't help but reflect that far too often those of us who live in America have *everything except happiness.* Those women who had so relatively little of the world's goods had *nothing but happiness.* The reason: their faith in the Lord and that He would provide for them.

Indeed, the answer to meeting life's challenges head-on is and always will be having a personal witness that Jesus is the Christ, our Savior and Redeemer, our Elder Brother who when called upon premortally said, "Here am I, send me," and who then fulfilled His atoning mission perfectly and completely.

Hence Moroni's plea, as he bid farewell to his brethren, knowing he would not meet them again until they met before the judgment-seat of Christ: "I would commend you to seek this Jesus of whom the prophets and apostles have written, that the grace of God the Father, and also the Lord Jesus Christ, and the Holy Ghost, which beareth record of them, may be and abide in you forever" (Ether 12:41).

It is seeking a personal witness that Jesus is the Christ, and committing to follow Him with all our hearts, that will bring to pass the glorious promise contained in the hymn of the exodus west:

> *Why should we mourn or think our lot is hard?*
> *'Tis not so; all is right.*
> *Why should we think to earn a great reward*
> *If we now shun the fight?*
> *Gird up your loins; fresh courage take.*
> *Our God will never us forsake;*
> *And soon we'll have this tale to tell—*
> *All is well! All is well!*
>
> (Hymns, *no. 30*)

All *is* well when our most compelling focus is following Jesus Christ.

Thomas Paine's *The American Crisis,* penned on December 23, 1776, as a powerful summons to American patriotism, could just as well have been written to describe our experience in mortality. "These are the times that try men's souls," he wrote. "The summer soldier and the sunshine patriot will, in this crisis, shrink from the service of his country, but he that stands it now deserves the love and thanks of man and woman. Tyranny, like hell, is not easily conquered; yet we have this consolation with us, that the harder the conflict, the more glorious the triumph. What we obtain too cheap, we esteem too lightly."

The application for us is obvious: These *are* the times that try men's souls, meaning we are living in the toughest of all tough days. And clearly, "sunshine followers" of Jesus Christ will inevitably shrink from the service of our Father and His Son during the crisis of our era. But those who withstand the battering of Satan and his forces; those who resist the untruths, deceptions, and evils being promulgated on street corners and billboards and websites around the world; will have the thanks not only of their fellow travelers attempting to walk the straight and narrow path but of Him whom they are seeking to follow. For it's true, hell is *not* easily conquered. Yet we may be consoled by the realization that the harder the conflict, the more glorious the triumph.

Truly, the riches of eternity may be ours (see D&C 38:39). For the Lord "delight[s] to honor those who serve [him] in righteousness and in truth unto the end. Great shall be their reward and eternal shall be their glory" (D&C 76:5–6).

Our challenge is to be able to say, as my nephew and nieces did that evening when one snafu after another interfered with our flight to Nauvoo: "Are you kidding, of course we still want to go. This is an adventure!" And, "Don't you get it, Aunt Sheri, if life were easy, it wouldn't be hard."

President Hinckley voiced essentially the same perspective when he told the young adults of the Church: "All of us have problems. We face them every day. How grateful I am that we have difficult things to wrestle with. They keep us young, if that is possible. They keep us alive. They keep us going. They keep us humble. They pull us down to our knees to ask the God of heaven for help in solving them. Be grateful for your problems, and know that somehow there will come a solution." And then he added words he has spoken frequently as President of the Church: "Just do the best you can, but be sure it is the very best. Then leave it in the hands of the Lord" ("An Evening with a General Authority," Church Educational System Fireside, 7 February 2003).

Even during those days when the challenges in front of us seem more intense and demanding than we have the capacity or stamina to handle, a personal testimony of Jesus Christ and an understanding of the power that lies within His gospel will make it possible for us to do our best. Our *very* best.

Chapter Two

THE LORD WILL CARRY OUR BURDENS, BUT NOT OUR BAGGAGE

Last fall I arrived in New York City late one evening for a crucial meeting the next morning. I was dead to the world when at 3:00 A.M. a fire alarm jolted me out of bed. As I prepared to dash out of the room, I was overcome with a wave of reality . . . and vanity. I don't look that great at 3:00 A.M. What if I couldn't get back to my room? How could I go to the meeting in flat hair and sweats? Quickly I threw clothes in my suitcase, grabbed my briefcase, and bolted out the door. For an instant I wondered if I should just leave my luggage behind. But I was going down. How hard could that be? I had failed, however, to factor in one *minor* detail: I was on the 44th floor.

The fire escape quickly filled with smoke and bathrobed guests, all of us heading down the stairs as fast as we could. Funniest thing, I was the *only one* carrying luggage. After a few floors my legs started to throb, then shake, then *scream* with pain. When I thought I couldn't take another step, I looked up to see that we were only on the 21st floor. But there weren't many options. If I dropped my bags or slowed down to rest, I would block the escape and put others at risk. I had no choice but to keep moving.

It was unbelievably grueling as I forced my muscles to keep going when they'd long since signaled that they were worn out. Somehow I made it down—but at a high price. Because there was one more small detail about this flight to safety: I was recovering from surgery on my left knee, so I forced the other knee to bear the brunt of the pounding— 1,232 stairs straight down (yes, 28 steps per floor), carrying 40 pounds of luggage. The escapade shredded my right knee, and I subsequently had to have surgery on that knee, from which the recovery was slow and painful. The moral of this pathetic story? When you have to evacuate your hotel, *leave your baggage in the room!*

That trip down 44 flights of stairs was a lot like our trip through mortality. It was scary—there were moments of sheer fear. It was more grueling and painful than I could have ever imagined. And even when I thought I couldn't take one more step, I had to keep going. Sound familiar?

But the trip didn't need to be as hard as I made it. I should have grabbed my laptop, phone, and scriptures—because each one helps me communicate—and left everything else behind (well, except maybe my makeup). Likewise, on this jaunt through mortality we've simply got to leave our baggage behind, because our spiritual joints can't take the pounding.

When I speak of baggage, I'm not talking about burdens. Burdens are part of the mortal experience—the burdens that come with unfulfilled expectations, with disappointment and heartache, with affliction and wavering faith. Loneliness can be a burden. Emotional wounds can be burdens. Heavy assignments from the Lord can feel like burdens. And certainly, sin creates burdens. But the Savior atoned precisely so we wouldn't have to carry our burdens alone. He knew they'd be too heavy for us. Thus His entreaty, "Come unto me, all ye that . . . are *heavy laden,* and I will give you rest. Take my yoke upon you, . . . For my yoke is easy, and my burden is light" (Matthew 11:28–30; emphasis added).

He who "descended below all things, in that he comprehendeth all things" (D&C 88:6) has the power to lift our burdens. "For we have not an high priest [meaning Christ] which cannot be touched with the feeling of our infirmities; but was in all points tempted like as we are, yet [was] without sin. Let us therefore come boldly unto the throne of grace, that we may obtain mercy, and find grace to help in time of need" (Hebrews 4:15–16). Alma promised that if we will plant the Word, or Christ, in our hearts and nourish it with our faith, God will "grant unto [us] that [our] burdens may be light, through the joy of his Son" (Alma 33:23). God the Father is the giver of all heavenly and eternal gifts—gifts He reserves for those who follow His Son.

Burdens have the potential to exalt us, but baggage just weighs us down and wears us out.

When we cast our burden upon the Lord, He sustains us either by helping us carry the burden or by ridding us of it entirely. Alma's people experienced this when their burdens "were made light; yea, the Lord did *strengthen* them that they could bear up their burdens with ease." The result: They submitted cheerfully and with patience to the will of the Lord. Ultimately "so great was their faith and their patience" that the Lord delivered them out of bondage (Mosiah 24:14–16; emphasis added).

Baggage, however, is another matter entirely. Burdens

have the potential to exalt us, but baggage just weighs us down and wears us out. When we don't repent, sin becomes baggage. Natural-man behaviors that we aren't ready to give up become baggage. Worry, jealousy, and guilt are baggage. An unforgiving heart, anger, regret, and pride are baggage. Resentment, the desire to retaliate, fear, and insecurity create unbearable baggage. We choose whether or not to pick up baggage, and Satan loves nothing more than loading us down like pack mules.

As architect of the greatest westward migration in U.S. history, Brigham Young knew full well how great a liability baggage could be: "If the Saints do not now appreciate the wisdom of taking the smallest practicable amount of luggage, they will before they have hauled it far on the plains" (*Millennial Star,* 18 [1856]: 123).

Just like our pioneer forebears who made the trek across the plains, if we don't want to carry any more than we have to through mortality, we've got to get rid of the baggage. The best manuals on baggage disposal, as well as on learning how to cast our burdens upon the Lord, are the scriptures, which are filled with truth and light. "And he that receiveth light, and continueth in God, receiveth more light; and that light groweth brighter and brighter until the perfect day" (D&C 50:24).

It was a scripture that prompted a fourteen-year-old boy

to kneel in a grove of trees in upstate New York and ask which church was true. In other words, a scripture triggered the Restoration. It was while Joseph and Sidney Rigdon were contemplating verses in the gospel of John that the "eyes of [their] understandings . . . were opened, and the glory of the Lord shone round about, And [they] beheld the glory of the Son, on the right hand of the Father, and received of his fulness" (D&C 76:19–20). It was as President Joseph F. Smith pondered verses from the New Testament that the eyes of his understanding were opened and he saw Christ ministering among the righteous dead (see D&C 138:11–12).

Indeed, the scriptures are a magnificent conduit of light, or personal revelation—which is why they are the ultimate latter-day survival manual. The pressures, disappointments, and quandaries of life would have crushed me long ago if it weren't for my scriptures pointing the way. I think of a recent episode when as I went to bed I was consumed with worry about a certain stewardship. But in the middle of the night I awoke with a scriptural promise in my mind: "Let us cheerfully do all things that lie in our power; and then may we stand still, with the utmost assurance, to see the salvation of God, and for his arm to be revealed" (D&C 123:17). The word *cheerfully* seemed underlined in my mind—a message to shake off the sheer fear that had gripped me and was weighing me down. Beyond that, I knew I was expected to do all I could and then to be at peace and leave the rest to the Lord.

The scriptures can help us with both our burdens and our baggage if we'll learn how to mine them for answers to every life situation and dilemma. To illustrate, let's unpack what they teach us about a particularly insidious kind of baggage—our sometimes ill treatment of each other—and what to do about it.

Years ago I attended a fireside at which a General Authority asked the audience how to tell if someone is a true follower of Jesus Christ. The chapel full of adults responded with a chalkboard full of answers, none of which was the one he was looking for. Finally he wiped the board clean and said something I've never forgotten: "Observation and personal experience have taught me that the way you can tell if someone is truly converted to Jesus Christ is by how that person treats others."

His answer surprised me. In fact—and this will reveal something about my level of spiritual maturity at the time—I didn't buy it. I immediately flipped open my scriptures and began to search for evidence to prove him wrong. But as it turns out, the doctrine that you can identify true followers of Jesus Christ by how they treat others is *every-where* in the scriptures.

When the Pharisees asked the Savior which was the

greatest commandment, He responded, "Thou shalt love the Lord thy God with all thy heart. . . . This is the first and great commandment. And the second is like unto it, Thou shalt love thy neighbor as thyself. On these two commandments hang *all* the law and the prophets" (Matthew 22:36–40; emphasis added).

All the laws of God hang on whether or not we love Him above all else, and then love each other as ourselves? Apparently so. The Apostle Paul taught the Romans that "he that loveth one another hath *fulfilled* the law" (Romans 13:8; emphasis added). The Savior Himself declared that "by this shall all men know that ye are my disciples, if ye have love one to another" (John 13:35). And after He visited this continent and converted *everyone*, "there was no contention in the land, *because* of the love of God which did dwell in the hearts of the people" (4 Nephi 1:15; emphasis added).

Alma offered perhaps the most succinct definition in all of scripture of the covenant that followers of Jesus Christ make at baptism when they pledge to become His people: True followers promise to bear one another's burdens, mourn with those that mourn, and comfort those that stand in need of comfort (see Mosiah 18:8–9).

In fact, I can't find *any* major scriptural sermon that isn't devoted *in large part* to our relationships with each other, with none more compelling than the Savior's sermons on both mounts. What did He teach the Nephites during His short time with them? Agree with your adversary quickly; if someone smites you on the right cheek, turn the other; if someone sues you for your coat give him your cloak also; if you're asked to go a mile, go two; love your enemies; bless those who curse you; do good to those who hate you; pray for them who despitefully use you. (See 3 Nephi 12:39, 40, 41, 44.) It's terrific material for a Sunday School lesson, but not very easy to do on a Tuesday afternoon when someone you care about or with whom you work regularly has hurt you for the umpteenth time. Further, in modern revelation the Savior added, "I, the Lord, will forgive whom I will forgive, but of you it is required to forgive all men" (D&C 64:10).

To take this another step, consider the reaction of men and women who have had conversion experiences. After the remarkable transformation of the sons of Mosiah, their thoughts turned immediately to the Lamanites, for they "could not bear that any human soul should perish" (Mosiah 28:3). After Enos's all-night conversion experience, he "began to feel a desire for the welfare of [his] brethren . . . ; wherefore [he] did pour out [his] whole soul unto God for them" (Enos 1:9).

Why such immediate concern for others by those who

are converted to the Lord Jesus Christ? And why such emphasis by the Lord on loving, forgiving, and resolving conflict? Why did the Lord declare that He can forgive whom He chooses, but we are required to forgive everyone? (See D&C 64:9–10.) Because He knew that behavior that injures our brothers and sisters, even when it feels justified, loads us down with trip-around-the-world-size baggage, baggage we can't carry without wrecking, even shredding, our spiritual joints.

How we respond to these injunctions is crucial, as the Master explained when He taught the Nephites: "If ye . . . *desire* to come unto me, . . . Go thy way unto thy brother, and *first* be reconciled to thy brother, and *then* come unto me with full purpose of heart, and I will receive you" (3 Nephi 12:23–24; emphasis added).

In other words, it's not possible to come unto Christ with *all* of our hearts (see Mormon 9:27) if our hearts are

> *Behavior that injures our brothers and sisters, even when it feels justified, loads us down with trip-around-the-world-size baggage, baggage we can't carry without wrecking our spiritual joints.*

tied in knots with envy or anger or resentment or pride. It's not possible to have a mighty change of heart, such that "we have no more disposition to do evil, but to do good continually" (Mosiah 5:2), if we're harboring grudges. It's not possible to give our hearts to God when they're laden with baggage. And yet, all the Lord really wants from us is our hearts. He said so in just those words: "For I, the Lord, require the hearts of the children of men" (D&C 64:22). Thus, if we are to keep the second commandment and love each other with a kind of love the natural man doesn't understand, we must love God first, with *all* our hearts. There is a word for this kind of love. Our Father and His Son call it *charity* (see Ether 12:33–34).

Charity is the pure love of Christ, and not only will it endure forever but its power to change and heal and transform us is limitless and eternal.

Chapter Three

OUR CHARITY
SOMETIMES FAILETH

Nephi saw in vision that the pure love of Christ, or charity, is "most desirable above all things" (1 Nephi 11:22). And his father, Lehi, described the unspeakable reach and power of this love: "I have beheld his glory," he recorded, "and I am encircled about eternally in the arms of his love" (2 Nephi 1:15). Joseph Smith did also, as he described in his 1832 account of the First Vision: "My Soul was filled with love and for many days I could rejoice with great joy" (Larry E. Dahl and Donald Q. Cannon, eds., *Encyclopedia of Joseph Smith's Teachings*, 254).

The Prophet Joseph declared that "it is natural for females to have feelings of charity—you are now placed in a situation where you can act according to those sympathies which God has planted in your bosoms." He then promised, "If you live up to these principles . . . the angels cannot be restrain'd from being your associates" (Andrew F. Ehat and Lyndon W. Cook, eds., *Words of Joseph Smith*, 117).

Our Father gifted His daughters in particular with the nature to nurture, encourage, and bear with one another, knowing that these gifts—this inclination toward charity— would be vital to all mankind. President Gordon B. Hinckley has referred to the women of the Church as the "*one bright shining hope* in a world . . . marching toward moral self-destruction" (Worldwide Leadership Training Broadcast, 10 January 2004; emphasis added). The women of the Church are the hope of the world *precisely* because it is not possible to limit the influence of a woman of God who is filled with the pure love of Christ. For that matter, the same is true of men. It is not possible to limit the influence of a man of God who bears the holy priesthood and who is filled with the pure love of Christ.

Satan knows this, and he hates followers of Christ for it. We are among his greatest nightmares because he knows he cannot limit our influence unless he can neutralize our respective natures. So, if he can get us to break the law of chastity, or develop an addiction, or become consumed with or blinded by the world, he laughs. When he seduces a man or a woman of God, he not only neutralizes those individuals but is poised to infiltrate their families.

If we don't fall for blatant tactics, however, he resorts to more subtle schemes, hoping to weigh us down with baggage that obscures our divine nature and causes us to buckle spiritually under the load. He tries to get us to judge, gossip, envy, resent, and punish those we could otherwise be nurturing. He is particularly fond of what could be called the Three C's: competing, comparing, and categorizing.

Why do we compete with each other? If we all had the capacity to work at our peak every day to build the kingdom, which none of us have, there would still be more to do, more to accomplish, more to get done, more people to influence. Why do we not therefore cheer for each other's gifts, contributions, and sincere efforts to make a difference in the world? Why do we make comparisons that are never fair? Why do we have an insatiable urge to label and categorize everyone when no one can be defined by a one-dimensional category?

We're not supposed to be alike. We weren't given the same gifts. None of us were given all of the gifts of God, but we were each given at least one spiritual gift (see D&C 46:11). And the reason seems obvious: The Lord needs a full spectrum of talent consecrated to His work. He also wants us to work together, rejoicing in each other's strengths and together compensating for each other's weaknesses. That is why comparing, competing, and categorizing—traps we seem to fall into naturally and repeatedly—are deadly.

Charity is the antidote for every baggage-breeding behavior. It is what lifts us above telestial living.

Behaviors such as these result from strategies forged in the bowels of hell by Lucifer himself. Lest you think this an overstatement, remember what the Risen Lord told the Nephites: "He that hath the spirit of contention is not of me, but is of the devil, who is the father of contention, and he stirreth up the hearts of men to contend with anger, one with another" (3 Nephi 11:29). And to our dispensation the Lord declared, "If ye are not one ye are not mine" (D&C 38:27).

Elder Cree-L Kofford said this in a classic general conference address: "Have you noticed how easy it is to cross over the line and find fault with other people? . . . Mercy for me, justice for everyone else is a much too common addiction. . . . There are those among us who would recoil in horror at the thought of stealing another person's money or property but who don't give a second thought to stealing another person's good name or reputation" (*Ensign,* May 1999, 82).

Charity is the antidote for every baggage-breeding behavior. It is what lifts us above telestial living.

I've seen charity in action time and again, in countless settings and cultures. One experience is indicative of many others. At age thirty-two, I was called to serve in a stake Relief Society presidency, and the three of us bonded quickly as the dearest of friends. Because of my work schedule and the large families of the president and other counselor, we held presidency meetings on Tuesdays at the unearthly hour of 5:30 A.M.

One morning, the president raised an issue that for some reason set me off. I climbed on my own Rameump-tom, delivered a tirade, and left in a huff. But as I drove away and headed toward work, my heart sank. I couldn't believe I'd responded to my friends that way, and I was desperate to apologize. But I felt as if I needed to do so in person, which I determined to do that very night.

Finally evening came. I stopped at home briefly to pick up something, only to have the doorbell ring. There stood my two friends, casseroles in hand. The mothers of fifteen children between them had brought me, the mother of none, dinner. I'll never forget what they said: "This morning wasn't like you. You must be under a lot of pressure. We thought dinner might make you feel better." Tears flowed as I apologized, and our friendship grew instantly stronger. Imagine what they could have been saying all day. "That little brat. She's not even married, what does she know? She's lucky to even be in this presidency." They could have whipped themselves into a lather and punished me for days.

But they didn't. They didn't gossip. They didn't judge. They *did* give me the benefit of the doubt. That day I saw what charity looks like. Charity was not, by the way, the casseroles. It was my friends' gentle handling of my mistake, and their willingness to assume the best and step forward to soothe feelings and emotions.

The Prophet Joseph declared that "nothing is so much calculated to lead people to forsake sin as to take them by the hand and watch over them with tenderness. When persons manifest the least kindness and love to me, O what pow'r it has over my mind" (Ehat and Cook, *Words of Joseph Smith,* 123). My friends took me by the hand and showed me a better way.

I imagine each of us can think of times when we didn't handle things very well. Why do we sometimes gossip and jump to unfair conclusions when we *never* have all the facts? Why do we get jealous when others succeed or get something we want? Why do we sometimes pout and set up silent competitions with each other? Why do we even at times attempt to sabotage someone else—usually all while justifying our behavior in our minds in some way? There are times when I wonder if the final judgment will be a breeze compared with what we put each other through here on earth! Our Father did not intend for His children to wrench each other's heartstrings.

I fear that *our* charity sometimes faileth. One wonders if the Prophet Joseph agreed. As just one way of demonstrating this, I cannot find even one address of the many he delivered to the Relief Society where he didn't implore the sisters to treat each other better. Here are just a few examples:

"Put a double watch over the tongue. . . . The tongue is an unruly member—hold your tongues about things of no moment—a little tale will set the world on fire. . . . Don't do more hurt than good, with your tongues—be pure in heart" (*Teachings of the Prophet Joseph Smith*, 239).

"As females possess refined feelings and sensitiveness, they are also subject to overmuch zeal, which must ever prove dangerous, and cause them to be rigid in a religious capacity—[they] should be armed with mercy, notwithstanding the iniquity among us" (Alma P. Burton, ed., *Discourses of the Prophet Joseph Smith*, 88–89).

"Don't be limited in your view with regard to your neighbors' virtues, but be limited toward your own virtues, and not think yourselves more righteous than others; you must enlarge your souls toward others if you [w]ould do like Jesus" (Ehat and Cook, *Words of Joseph Smith*, 118).

And lest the men think they get off the hook, he also spoke of great big Elders, as he called them, who had "caused him much trouble" by claiming and teaching his revelations as their own. He said he had been "trampled underfoot by aspiring Elders, for all were infected with that spirit," then added a warning to the sisters that "the same aspiring disposition will be in this society, and must be guarded against" (Ehat and Cook, *Words of Joseph Smith*, 116; see also *Contributor*, vol. 3, October 1881–September 1882, 322; *Teachings of the Prophet Joseph Smith*, 225).

Further, Joseph was not the only prophet in this dispensation to address this topic. As just one additional example of many that could be cited, during those stressful days at Winter Quarters, Brigham Young counseled his beleaguered band to "cease to contend one with another; cease to speak evil one of another. . . . Let your words tend to edifying one another" (D&C 136: 23–24).

For years I have pondered and prayed about charity—in part because more than twenty years of service in various Relief Society presidencies has drawn me to Moroni 7 again and again. But further, many experiences during recent years have caused me to think more deeply about charity—

what it really is, what it can do for us, and why such superlatives are used to describe it.

I think of an African-American sister who called me in distress after her first Sunday in a new ward where a woman told her, "This is a white ward; yours is across town." I was shocked to hear that something of that nature could still take place. Where might she have turned for a friend that day? I think of a couple who had to move to escape persistent condemnation from fellow Saints after their son took his life because he could no longer cope with same-gender attraction. They mourned alone. I think of a friend whose hopes for ten children were dashed by illness. She called in tears after overhearing friends say, "I wonder why she and her husband only had one child?" My friend's response? "We wonder too."

I think of another woman who recently called me. "Can you help me?" she pleaded, reaching out in what felt like desperation to someone she had never met. "Our Gospel Doctrine teacher keeps teaching that converts aren't as worthy as those born in the covenant. Is that true? Can I never feel fully worthy before the Lord?" Hmmm. Technically speaking, the Prophet Joseph was a convert. As were Brigham and Heber, Parley and Eliza. No doubt this instructor was simply in error, having apparently not noticed how many times the Lord promises to give all He has to *everyone* who qualifies through his or her faithfulness. But the effect on this woman was the same as it would have been if the slight had been intentional.

We probably all relate to moments like these. I have found that being the somewhat recognizable president of a visible company (in the LDS culture) has its ups and downs. I was walking to my car after a Tabernacle Choir Christmas concert when a woman approached me and said, "Sister Dew, you're the president of Deseret Book, aren't you?" "Yes," I responded. "Well, I just want you to know that I *hate* the ads you're running on TV," she said with venom. Taken aback a little, I tried to sound calm as I answered, "Thank you, I'll pass that along to our marketing department." "No, I mean, I really hate those ads," she persisted. "Thank you," I said again, trying to reassure her that I truly would pass along her feedback. But she wasn't satisfied and kept on, "But how could you have let them run those ads? They're awful." At a loss to know how to make her feel better there in the parking lot, I simply thanked her again for her feedback and then walked on. I found myself wondering, though, what motivated such angry comments.

I was similarly perplexed when a recent symposium sponsored by an LDS-oriented periodical featured a session that evaluated my addresses, focusing particularly on my rhetoric and on whether or not I practiced what I preached.

When I listened to a recording of the presentation after the fact, I was amazed that people who had never met or talked with me could have developed an entire presentation in which they judged my motives and the intent of my heart. I was also interested in attitudes and feelings they attributed to me that were not at all true, and was particularly fascinated to learn that I had *chosen* to remain single so that I could have a more powerful voice. I guess there is no way they could have known—especially without asking me—about the thousands of hours (over three decades at latest count) I have spent fasting, in the temple, and on my knees pleading with the Lord for the blessing of marriage that seems to come so easily to so many.

Some experiences are far more painful, though, than brief encounters in parking lots or even symposium commentaries that come and go. As an example, in the summer of 2004, I was invited to offer an invocation at the Republican National Convention. My immediate reaction? "Thanks, but no thanks!" Though I have a deep patriotic streak, I'm not very political. I didn't want to worry about praying in such a non-prayerlike setting. I didn't want to go to New York City during the frenzy of a convention. It all sounded like a big hassle to me.

I was ready to phone with my regrets, but several questions nagged at me: What if this invitation had been divinely prompted? (There certainly wasn't any earthly explanation for it.) If I declined, would they ask another Church member to pray? What about the First Presidency's repeated counsel that we be involved citizens? (See First Presidency Letter, 28 October 2003.) Furthermore, was it ever wrong to pray? And what about the tired media perception that LDS women are oppressed creatures who can't think for themselves? Was this a chance for the world to see that, yes, LDS women pray—even in public?

So I reluctantly accepted. I worked very hard to craft a way to acknowledge the Savior without offending those who didn't believe in Him. The prayer I offered was nonpartisan. Ironically, I prayed that we might live without acrimony . . . and then flew home to an avalanche of criticism.

Because one media report implied that I was a Democrat, I got blasted by both appalled Republicans (that I could possibly be a Democrat) and insulted Democrats (that I had prayed at a Republican event). (By the way, I've never been asked my party affiliation at a temple recommend interview.) One letter to the editor in a local newspaper began, "Shame on Sheri Dew," and then tore me apart. The criticism was painful and embarrassing. I have second-guessed giving that prayer a hundred times. Frankly, it may have been a mistake. But I feel at peace about one thing—that the Lord, at least, will judge me on the intent of my heart. Which is why He reserves judgment for Himself. Only He can see the whole of any picture, including what's in our hearts.

As an aside, there were those who found humor in the entire situation, as did a treasured friend who e-mailed me afterward with this: "My brother and I were feeling sad that we didn't get to hear your prayer or see you at the convention. He hit on the idea of going to Google to see if we could find a copy of your prayer. I'm sending along what we found, and he's wondering if this is REALLY the prayer you offered."

> *We are grateful for the music which has stirred every*
>   *fiber of our being.*
> *We know that this is the right place to be.*
> *We believe that thou hast separated us from our*
>   *brethren, and we do not believe in their foolish*
>   *traditions.*
> *We are so glad we are not bound down to the plat-*
>   *form of our opponents.*
> *But we believe that we're supposed to be elected, while*
>   *all around us will be disappointed.*
> *Nevertheless and notwithstanding, truth shall*
>   *prevail.*
> *The elephant shall not lie down with the . . . uh . . .*
>   *donkey in this world or the world to come.*

> *We know without a shadow of a doubt who Thou*
> *desires to be president.*
> *Bless the poor and the needy, the sick and the*
> *afflicted, and those associated with the wrong*
> *candidate.*
> *We hope all those who are not here this time will be*
> *here next time.*
> *Take us to our various homes in safety.*

Humor can take the sting out of situations where charity is not present. Humor can help us see, sometimes, just how far afield we may have strayed in terms of how we are viewing (and too often judging and commenting upon) the actions of those around us. Because it can be discouraging to do your best in a difficult situation, only to have your motives and judgment questioned by people who weren't there and under pressure to make the right decision at the right time.

No one in our dispensation has been more harshly or unfairly judged than has the Prophet Joseph, and such assessments continue to the current day. Certainly Joseph had his own foibles. Some living in his day could see past them; others could not. To this day I marvel at those who insist on trying to identify any little flaw, assuming that such a revelation might throw his prophetic calling in question.

And yet, think about what he dealt with. The Lord put the Restoration in the hands of a teenager. Further, Joseph was only twenty-four, a young adult, the day the Church was organized on April 6, 1830. Think about what he did— against unbelievable odds. This young boy prophet never went to a youth conference or EFY, never had a bishop's interview or a supportive priests quorum advisor, never went to seminary or institute, never attended a Church dance or activity. Yet while some in his day focused on the magnificence of what he was accomplishing, others couldn't see past his mortal, human, young-adult mistakes, made while charting a course through completely unknown territory.

There are similarities for us. Some of those we bump into along this life's path are able to see past our foibles and follies, realizing that what we are trying to do is actually quite remarkable. Set against the intense backdrop of the last days, we have been sent here to do things no other group of men or women in history have been required to do in quite the same way and under quite the same degree of pressure. How unfortunate it is, then, when we focus heavily on each other's mistakes or moments of poor judgment!

Now, two cautions. First, none of us handles things perfectly all the time, which is just one of the reasons I love Lehi's wife, Sariah, whose faith wavered a bit when fear for her sons momentarily overcame her confidence in her husband and in the Lord. And second, we are *expected* to judge good from evil if we are to protect ourselves and those we love. The Holy Ghost (see 1 Nephi 13:37) and the Spirit of Christ which is "given to every man" help us do so, for we "may know good from evil; and the way to judge is as plain, that [we] may know with a perfect knowledge, as the daylight is from the dark night" (Moroni 7:15–16). Further, turning the other cheek does not mean allowing others to abuse us, and particularly it does not mean we should allow others to abuse us again and again.

> *Turning the other cheek does not mean allowing others to abuse us. What we are not authorized to do, however, is make judgments that convict, sentence, and execute one another.*

What we are *not* authorized to do, however, is make judgments that convict, sentence, and execute one another. In each case they are violations of the law of charity.

Perhaps more telling, such judgments indicate that we don't understand what charity really is, where it comes from, and what it can do in our lives.

An unnamed author is reported to have said, "In essentials, let there be unity; in non-essentials, liberty; and in all things, charity" (as quoted by B. H. Roberts in Conference Report, October 1912, 30). In other words, in the things that really matter—our covenants, the commandments, and following the prophet—we need to be completely united. In the non-essentials, we have our agency to handle things as we see fit. But in all things, regardless of whether we make the same choices or not, we are to treat each other with dignity and respect, both of which are evidences of charity in our hearts and lives.

Chapter Four

IT IS POSSIBLE TO CHANGE, REALLY CHANGE

There is but one cure for the ills that infect our personalities, our emotions, and our behavior—the kinds of ills that sometimes seem impossible to heal. But it is possible to change. *Really* change. The cure for the ills with which we deal is the pure love of Christ. But how do we get it? And how do we get to the point where we can pray for and truly love those who wound us?

Mormon taught us *exactly* what to do: We are to "pray unto the Father with all the energy of heart," meaning the kind of energy we put forth when we are desperate for help, desperate to feel peace or solace, that we may be "filled with this love, which he [meaning our Father] hath *bestowed* upon all who are *true followers* of his Son, Jesus Christ" (Moroni 7:48; emphasis added).

Charity is a bestowal, a gift from our Father. To whom? To *all*—the word *all* is *always* the word used to indicate those who have the potential to receive what the Father has agreed to bless His children with—who are *true followers* of Jesus Christ. Not perfect followers, or size-5 followers, or mother-of-six followers, or chairman of the board followers, or Most Valuable Player followers. But *true* followers, meaning *all* those who come unto the Lord with *all* their hearts and love Him with *all* their might, mind, and strength (see Mormon 9:27; Moroni 10:32). *True followers.*

Charity is not an emotion or an action. It is not something we feel or do. Charity is who the Savior is. It is His most defining and dominant attribute.

There is no greater way to worship the Father than by following and serving His Son. The gift of charity is bestowed only upon those who follow the Son. It is the greatest of all the gifts of the Spirit. But it may be the most underestimated and even the least understood. We tend to define charity as something we do or feel, but in our Father's vernacular, charity means much more. It is the word He uses to describe the character, the nature, the very essence of His Son.

Charity is not an emotion or an action. It is not some-thing we feel or do. *Charity is who the Savior is.* It is His most defining and dominant attribute. It is what enabled Him to endure the Garden and the cross for you and me. It is one of the things that makes Him God. Thus, when we plead for the gift of charity, we aren't asking for lovely feelings toward someone who bugs us or someone who has injured or wounded us. We are actually pleading for our very natures to be changed, for our character and disposition to become more and more like the Savior's, so that we literally feel as He would feel and thus do what He would do. That explains why Mormon said that when the Savior appears, those who have been gifted with charity "shall be like him," for they shall "see him as he is" (Moroni 7:48).

It also explains why Paul told the Corinthians that even if they spoke with the tongue of angels and had the gift of prophecy and understood all the mysteries and had the faith to move mountains, if they didn't have charity, they were nothing. It explains why he told them that even if they gave all their goods to the poor, that wasn't charity either. Helping those in need may very well be a manifestation of true charity, but it is not charity itself.

Paul concluded his sermon on charity with the statement

that of faith, hope, and charity, the greatest is charity (see 1 Corinthians 13:1–3, 13). The implications of that declaration are spiritually staggering. Could charity possibly be greater than faith in the Lord Jesus Christ? Or greater than hope in the Atonement? Or greater than hope for happiness in this life or hope for a better world and a place at the right hand of God (see Ether 12:4)? Yes, because charity defines who and what we are seeking to become. Charity defines the nature of godliness. Paul taught the Colossians that charity was the "bond of perfectness" (Colossians 3:14). Said the Prophet Joseph, "Love is one of the chief characteristics of Deity, and ought to be manifested by those who aspire to be the sons [and I would add daughters] of God" (*History of the Church,* 4:227).

Very simply, without charity we cannot enter the celestial kingdom, because if our natures have not become defined by charity, then we won't be like our Father and His Son. It's as simple, and as profound, as that.

For charity changes us. It transforms us. It is as a healing balm. When we plead with all the energy of our hearts to be filled with the pure love of Christ, the increasing, continual bestowal of charity not only changes our natures, it heals us from the emotional and other wounds created by the buffetings we experience in this lone and dreary world—

wounds such as insecurity and jealousy, resentment and fear, a propensity for anger and an unforgiving heart. The healing power of charity, bestowed by our Father and made possible by the Atonement of Jesus Christ, can make it virtually impossible for us even to feel emotions common to the natural man.

President George Q. Cannon taught this: "Have I imperfections? I am full of them. What is my duty? To pray to God to give me the gifts that will correct these imperfections. If I am an angry man, it is my duty to pray for charity, which suffereth long and is kind. Am I an envious man? It is my duty to seek for charity, which envieth not. . . . No man ought to say, 'Oh, I cannot help this; it is my nature.' He is not justified in it, for the reason that God has promised to give strength to correct these things, and to give gifts that will eradicate them. . . . That is the design of God concerning His Church. He wants His Saints to be perfected in the truth. For this purpose He gives these gifts, and bestows them upon those who seek after them, in order that they may be a perfect people upon the face of the earth, notwithstanding their many weaknesses, because God has promised to give the gifts that are necessary for their perfection" (*Millennial Star* 56 [1894]: 260–61).

I repeat: The healing power of charity, bestowed by our Father, made possible by the Atonement of Jesus Christ, and delivered to us by the Holy Ghost, can make it virtually impossible even to feel emotions common to the natural man. In fact, charity can drop-kick the natural man (and woman) right out of play.

There is no way to quantify or limit the sustaining and reforming power of the pure love of Christ, which is why we can literally change as our natures become more and more like His.

C. S. Lewis wrote that as we begin to mature spiritually,

> *Charity can drop-kick the natural man (and woman) right out of play.*

we begin to notice, besides our particular sinful acts, our sinfulness; we begin to be alarmed not only about what we do, but about what we are. This may sound rather difficult, so I will try to make it clear from my own case. When I come to my evening prayers and try to reckon up the sins of the day, nine times out of ten the most obvious one is some sin against charity. I have sulked or snapped or sneered or snubbed or stormed. And the excuse that immediately springs to mind is that the provocation [against me] was so sudden and unexpected: I was caught off my guard, I had not time to collect myself. Now that may be an extenuating circumstance as regards those particular acts: they would obviously be worse if they had been deliberate and premeditated. On the other hand, surely what a man does when he is taken off his guard is the best evidence for what sort of a man he is? Surely what pops out before the man has time to put on a disguise is the truth. . . .

If there were rats in a cellar you are most likely to see them if you go in very suddenly. But the suddenness does not create the rats: it only prevents them from hiding. In the same way the suddenness of the provocation does not make me an ill-tempered man: it only shows me what an ill-tempered man I am. . . . And if (as I said before) what we are matters even more than what we do—if, indeed, what we do matters chiefly as evidence of what we are—then it follows that the change which I most need to undergo is a change that my own direct, voluntary efforts cannot bring about. . . . I cannot, by direct, moral effort, give myself new motives. After the first few steps in the Christian life we realise that everything which really needs to be done in our souls can be done only by God. (*Mere Christianity*, 164–65)

Again, charity is a bestowal from the Father to true followers of His Son. He and only He can change our hearts and our natures.

Now, becoming like the Savior—meaning, having our natures become like His—is not a quick or easy process. But we are admonished to "covet earnestly the best gifts" (1 Corinthians 12:31). The pure love of Christ is the best gift. It is to be coveted, sought after, and even craved. As we pray with all the energy we can muster to be filled with His love, our natures will gradually change, we will slowly become more and more like Him, and our actions and feelings will increasingly be *manifestations* of pure charity. Thus, charity is a healing, transforming balm—bestowed by the Father, applied by the Holy Ghost, to true followers of the Son—that will change our very nature as it purifies us.

Charity is a healing, transforming balm—bestowed by the Father, applied by the Holy Ghost, to true followers of the Son—that will change our very nature as it purifies us.

So on those days when we're not ready to stop being offended about something, not ready to forgive someone, still determined to give someone the silent treatment, and so on, what we're actually saying is, "Wait! I don't want to become more like the Savior today. Maybe tomorrow when I'm able to let go of some irritation or injustice." Perhaps those are the times when we need to pray the hardest, the times that make it clear that a change in behavior is not enough—that we *must* have a change in nature. As the Father applies the balm of charity to our hearts and souls, everything from emotional wounds to personality flaws can be healed and even transformed.

President Ezra Taft Benson described the process this way: "The Lord works from the inside out. The world works from the outside in. The world would take people out of the slums. Christ takes the slums out of the people, and then they take themselves out of the slums. The world would mold men by changing their environment. Christ changes men, who then change their environment. The world would shape human behavior, but Christ can change human nature" (in Conference Report, October 1985, 5).

There are countless examples of scriptural heroes and heroines whose natures are defined by charity. Pahoran's reaction to Moroni is one such vivid demonstration. On a particularly bad day, Captain Moroni, who had clearly had all the frustration he could take, wrote Pahoran, who was governor of the land, and chewed him out for his inadequate response to his armies. "Great has been your neglect towards us," Moroni lashed out. "Can you think to sit upon your thrones in a state of thoughtless stupor . . . ? Even they who have looked up to you for protection, yea, have placed you in a situation that ye might have succored them . . . [But] ye have withheld your provisions from them." He concluded with this denouncement: "Ye ought to have stirred yourselves more diligently for the welfare and the freedom of this people. . . . Could ye suppose that ye could sit upon your thrones, and because of the exceeding goodness of God ye could do nothing and he would deliver you?" (Alma 60:5–11).

Freeze frame. Think about the last time you were unjustly accused and condemned by someone you thought was your colleague and ally. How did you feel? More importantly, how did you respond? Were you tempted at all to retaliate? Now, consider the response of Pahoran, whose government had been under siege and thus had not been in a position to send provisions to Moroni's armies—and who therefore might have rightly been infuriated at the judgmental, condemning tone of Moroni's sizzling letter: "I do not joy in your great afflictions, yea, it grieves my soul," he replied. "In your epistle you have censured me, but it mattereth not; I am not angry, but do rejoice in the greatness of your heart" (Alma 61: 2, 9).

Note the similarities between Pahoran's behavior and the qualities identified by Mormon in his classic discourse on charity: "And charity *suffereth long*, and is *kind*, and envieth not, and is *not puffed up*, seeketh not her own, is *not easily provoked*, *thinketh no evil*, and *rejoiceth not in iniquity* but *rejoiceth in the truth*, *beareth all things*, believeth all things, hopeth all things, *endureth all things*" (Moroni 7:45; emphasis added).

Pahoran, like many others identified in the scriptures, was a true follower gifted with charity. Nevertheless, Elder Jeffrey R. Holland said that "true charity has been known only once. It is shown perfectly and purely in Christ's unfailing, ultimate, and atoning love for us. . . . Thus, the miracle of Christ's charity both saves and changes us. His atoning love saves us from death and hell . . . [and] transforms the soul, lifting it . . . to something far more noble, far more holy" (*Christ and the New Covenant*, 336–37).

Just like you, some days I do better than others. But many times in recent years I have found myself on my knees pleading for a bestowal of charity, pleading to respond as the Savior would rather than as my natural woman wanted or was inclined to, pleading to have my very nature changed so that I wasn't even capable of feeling certain negative or painful emotions anymore. And I testify that it is possible to truly forgive, possible to extend a hand to those who have maligned you, possible to feel old emotional wounds healing, and possible to change your response to difficult situations as you feel yourself slowly changing.

Realistically, from time to time we disappoint each other. But it really doesn't matter. Among the last verses Hyrum Smith read before leaving for Carthage was the counsel that if others didn't have charity, "it mattereth not unto thee, *thou* hast been faithful" (Ether 12:37; emphasis added). If we're serious about sanctification, we can expect to experience, though to a far lesser degree, what the Savior experienced—loneliness, false accusation, isolation, and the like. When those things happen, it doesn't matter, *if* we turn to the Lord for help rather than retaliating as the natural man or woman is inclined to do.

The Lord needs every one of us, and we need each other. A distinguishing feature of the gospel of Jesus Christ is that it makes His followers one.

Indeed, the Lord has admonished us to "lift up the hands which hang down, and strengthen the *feeble knees*" (D&C 81:5; emphasis added). Of all my many injuries—including ruptured disks and a separated shoulder—nothing has been as immobilizing or limiting as the injuries to my knees described in an earlier chapter. We each at some point have spiritually feeble knees and need to lean on others to steady and strengthen us. For "if any . . . among you be strong in the Spirit, let him take with him him that is weak, . . . that he may become strong also. . . . [For] the body hath need of *every* member, that all may be edified together" (D&C 84:106, 110; emphasis added).

The Lord needs every one of us, and we need each

other. A distinguishing feature of the gospel of Jesus Christ is that it makes His followers one. President George Q. Cannon declared that "there is no power on earth . . . that can shake . . . this people if they are only united. No matter what course we may take, so long as it is in righteousness, if we are united, we can stand against the world" (*Gospel Truth*, 205). The Prophet Joseph taught that "unity is strength. . . . Let the Saints of the Most High ever cultivate this principle, and the most glorious blessings must result, not only to them individually, but to the whole Church" (*History of the Church*, 4:227). And said President Gordon B. Hinckley, speaking directly to the women of the Church: "There is no other organization anywhere to match the Relief Society. If [its members] will be united and speak with one voice, their strength will be incalculable. We call upon the women of the Church to *stand together*" (Worldwide Leadership Training, 10 January 2004; emphasis added). When we stand together, we're far more able to build the kingdom.

After the Savior's ministry on this continent, there were no Lamanites "nor any manner of -ites, but they were in one, the children of Christ, and heirs to the kingdom of God" (4 Nephi 1:17). The Nephites later separated themselves into categories and classes, and look what it got them. Surely we can be smarter than they were. Their record has been preserved, at least in part, so that we won't fall prey to the same traps.

When we categorize each other—as single or married, active or inactive, affluent or of modest means, educated or not—we put up artificial boundaries that divide us. When I was twenty-nine I bought my first home and moved into a "regular" (meaning non-singles) ward. If I had stepped out of a spaceship in the Church parking lot that first Sunday, I wouldn't have been treated with any more suspicion. I was instantly labeled "single" and ignored.

The barriers melted away, though, when a sister bore her testimony in Relief Society and said how grateful she was for the unique perspective I brought to the ward. That was all it took—one friend who accepted me. In time, that one friend became thousands. I served eight years in the stake Relief Society presidency there—first as a counselor, and later as the president—which remains a treasured life experience. It didn't matter that almost everyone in that stake was married. There were no -ites among us.

Last summer I hiked part of Alaska's Chilkoot Trail, made famous by prospectors during the Klondike Gold Rush. It was five weeks after my first knee surgery, and though I wasn't yet at full strength, I was doing well enough to manage what was billed as a moderate hike. When our guide noticed my limp, I reassured her that I'd be fine. But as she instructed our group about what to do if we saw a bear, she looked over at me, laughed, and said to everyone, "You really only have to run faster than one other person. . . . Sorry, Sheri."

Contrast that with what I observed in the lobby of my charred hotel after spending a night on a curb in midtown Manhattan. Hundreds of tired guests waited in line for elevators—except one upset little boy who refused to get in line. The weary fire chief noticed, walked over and knelt down by the boy, and asked what was wrong. Through tears the boy said, "The building's on fire, and I'm afraid it's going to fall."

We each have to walk through life on our own, but no one should have to do it alone.

At that, the fireman put his arm around the boy and said, "There is nothing to be afraid of. I put out the fire myself. It's safe, or I wouldn't have let you come back inside. Will you go with me to your room?" They headed toward the elevator, hand in hand. Now, imagine if everyone who came within our sphere of influence knew that we had checked the area, that we had doused the flames, and that they were completely safe with us. We each have to walk through life on our own, but no one should have to do it alone.

My dear friends, *we've got to stand together.* We can't keep one commandment, one covenant, or any of our premortal promises without charity, meaning without our natures becoming more and more like Christ's. Imagine what would happen—in our families, our wards, our neighborhoods, everywhere—if we dumped some of our baggage, and if the comparing, competing, and categorizing stopped. The stopping can start now: with us. I invite you to identify one piece of baggage you want to get rid of. Plead with the Lord to change your heart about something or someone. Plead with Him to change your very nature in an area that has always plagued you. Then go to work. See what you are drawn to do. Right a wrong. Apologize or accept an apology. Give someone another chance. You'll be amazed how much better you feel as the baggage begins to fall away. There is no way to overestimate the strength we can be to one another as our natures increase in charity and we are drawn to bear one

> *There is no way to overestimate the strength we can be to one another as our natures increase in charity.*

another's burdens rather than load each other down with baggage.

Perhaps we don't always realize how powerful and uniquely sustaining our support can be, one for another. My first international trip as a member of the Relief Society general presidency was to eastern Canada, including meetings in Montreal's French-speaking stake. I loved those sisters instantly, and among other things told them I would soon be speaking in my first General Relief Society Meeting and that I was apprehensive about it. After the meeting, just as I was getting ready to leave, the stake Relief Society president gathered a group of women around me and told me they would pray for me the night of the General Relief Society Meeting. I was touched by their kindness, but then flew home and, frankly, forgot about their sweet promise.

The night of the meeting arrived, and I found myself on the stand in the Tabernacle, waiting my turn to walk to the podium. As the meeting progressed, I moved from apprehensive to nervous to all-out terrified, my heart pounding so hard that air wasn't getting into my lungs. "Please, Heavenly Father," I pleaded silently, "it will be important for me to be able to breathe." But it felt as though I was moving toward a complete meltdown.

Then, just before my turn, as I silently pleaded again for

help, the image of those women gathered around me in Montreal flashed through my mind and a feeling of calm washed over me from head to toes. Just seconds later, I stood and delivered my message—and was able to both breathe and talk.

We are to bear each other's burdens, even to absorb each other's burdens, but not to cause each other's burdens.

A few days later, a dear friend happened to be traveling to Montreal and was expecting to attend the French-speaking stake. I asked her to tell that stake Relief Society president what had happened to me while sitting on the stand in the Tabernacle. When she did, that good woman responded instantly, "We knew she would know! We knew Sister Dew would know we had prayed for her."

I marvel that it was the image of a group of women I had met only once and may never see again that the Holy Ghost chose to send me as He bestowed peace upon my anxious heart. Which leads me to ask, simply, Do we realize the impact we have upon each other? Do we realize the power we have to bless and heal and soothe and urge each other onward? No wonder the Apostle Paul wrote the

Corinthians: "I beseech you, . . . by the name of our Lord Jesus Christ, that ye all speak the same thing, and that there be no divisions among you; but that ye be perfectly joined together" (1 Corinthians 1:10). And similarly, the Lord admonished Joseph Smith to "let every man esteem his brother as himself and practise virtue and holiness before me. . . . Be one; and if ye are not one ye are not mine" (D&C 38:24, 27).

When the Lord assigned Peter Whitmer to be Oliver Cowdery's missionary companion, he taught Peter that he was serious about His followers bearing one another's burdens when he said, "And be you afflicted *in all his afflictions,* ever lifting up your heart unto me in prayer and faith for *his and your* deliverance" (D&C 30:6; emphasis added). The message seems clear: We are to bear each other's burdens, even to absorb each other's burdens, but not to cause each other's burdens.

Surely some of the sociality we enjoy here existed before. Perhaps that is why so many of us seem familiar to one another, and why we find it so easy to love one another. Surely we helped each other before. Surely we shouted encouragement from our various battle stations along the walls of our eternal fortress. Surely we taught and testified to each other and perhaps even promised to help each other when we met again on the foreign turf of mortality and were faced with the archenemy of all righteousness.

Brigham Young once wrote facetiously in a Church member's autograph book:

> *To live with Saints in Heaven is bliss and glory;*
> *To live with Saints on Earth is another story.*
> *(Barbara Neff Autograph Book)*

Oh, that we don't allow it to be so!

The Prophet Joseph warned the Relief Society that "the enemy will never get weary" (Ehat and Cook, *Words of Joseph Smith*, 131). So neither can we. The Lord will help us carry our burdens, but we can't expect to pack around extra baggage and have the stamina we need to win the real battle.

No finer group of women or men have ever walked this earth. That is doctrine. We are here now because our Father chose us to be here now. That is doctrine. There is no way to limit or measure the influence of a man or woman who is a true follower of Jesus Christ—a man or woman who craves the gift of charity because he or she is determined to slowly become more and more like the Son, to share His very nature. That is doctrine. For the more we become like Him, the more our actions, feelings, and efforts will never fail but will endure forever.

Let us therefore do as the Apostle Paul admonished and "lay aside every weight [including every piece of baggage], and . . . run with patience the race that is set before us, Looking unto Jesus the author and finisher of our faith; who for the joy that was set before him endured the cross" (Hebrews 12:1–2).

We can do it. I know we can.

Chapter Five

THE LAW OF CHASTITY DEFINES THE FAMILY

Iknow a little girl who was afraid of the dark. *Really* afraid of the dark. Even when she was old enough to attend grade school, nighttime terrified her. Every night, she and her mother went through a ritual designed to make her feel secure in her room. But inevitably, during the night, the girl would sneak into her parents' room and climb in bed with them, at which point her mother would carry her back to her room. Over a period of time, her mother used every argument and tactic she could think of to wean her daughter from the fear of sleeping all night in her own room. Often she would say something to this effect: "Honey, this is your room. You're safe here. Your father and I are just down the hall." And then she would usually add, "Heavenly Father is watching over you. You'll be just fine."

One night when the cycle repeated itself for the umpteenth time, the mother took her daughter back to her own room, reassuring her once again, "Honey, you're okay. Heavenly Father is watching over you." To which the little girl—who had obviously thought about this—instantly responded, "Mom, don't you know? Sometimes you just need someone with skin on."

It's true. Sometimes we just need to hug someone, reach out to someone, or have someone reach out to us. There is something to the notion of "contact comfort," which is one of the most natural and sustaining blessings, though per-haps overlooked in the rush of our busy lives, that occurs in a healthy family. Families consist of people with skin on—ideally, men and women, boys and girls, who care about us, love us, reach out to us, and sustain us. It doesn't matter if things haven't gone all that well on a particular day, or if we've just scored a resounding success, there is nothing quite like being able to come home at night into the embrace of loving, supportive family members and have them say, "You're going to be okay," or "Way to go! We're so proud of you!" As a girl I learned to listen for my mother to say, "Things will be fine," or "You can do it!" Interestingly, this many years later, when I hit a bump or a crisis, I still wait to hear those words of reassurance.

On a nearly endless number of occasions in recent years, I have been overwhelmed with anxiety over something that wasn't going terribly well or some assignment that far exceeded my capacity. Yet even such intense feelings can disappear after an evening with nieces and nephews who make me laugh and who remind me that there are things more important than work or worry. This is what happens when you're in the presence of people who love you for who you are—nothing more, nothing less. Suddenly, the anxieties and pressures of the day don't seem quite as suffocating, the problems quite as intense or even as important, for that matter. It helps to be with people who have skin on, people who are bound together by a bond that cannot be duplicated by any other gathering or organization.

And that is the case with the family. No other organization or entity can duplicate the family. And yet, almost incredibly, the family as we know it and as our Father in Heaven intended it to be is enduring the most deadly and consistent barrage of all time.

Most of us are perhaps not in a position to lead a parade or have a public forum in which to speak out. But we all have influence. We have influence with husbands and wives;

with children of our own or children we care about; with mothers and dads; with neighbors and friends; with the seventeen-year-olds we teach in Sunday School. Whatever our circle of involvement happens to be, we all have influence. And we all have people in our lives who look to us as a voice of authority. So when it comes to the family, and those things we see happening in our society that affect the family, what can we reasonably do about it? What do we need to understand and what steps can we take to shore up this most crucial of all institutions?

The issues that swirl around the family today are staggering in both their importance and implications. I grew up watching TV programs such as *The Andy Griffith Show* and *I Love Lucy* and *The Dick Van Dyke Show*, where Rob and Laura Petrie slept in twin beds. Though I haven't seen any of those programs recently, I doubt you could find even the most subtle sexual innuendo in any of their episodes, not to mention many other shows of that time period. It just wasn't there.

At the risk of appearing to promote television programs of a bygone era, I comment on this only to demonstrate that it's difficult *not* to notice the phenomenal moral deterioration taking place almost before our very eyes. That deterioration is often readily detected by examining virtually any form of media for messages about love, marriage, and family. Simply put, jamming the airwaves 24/7 today is programming that not only regularly dismantles the natural family but is often so sexually explicit that, had it aired thirty years ago, almost anyone would have classified the fare as pornography.

Little by little, and right in front of our eyes, the world is moving into dangerous territory with respect to the definition and protection of the traditional or natural family—which God has defined as mother, father, and children.

I have spoken and written to this topic a number of times before, but at the risk of repeating myself at least to some degree, I can't resist addressing it again because of my compelling concern. Issues related to the family are of such import that every one of us who understands our Father's Plan of Happiness needs to be well versed in what is taking place all around us, as well as prepared to do our part in stemming the tide of deterioration.

There are many recent developments, particularly in American society, that are individually wreaking havoc with the definition and protection of the traditional family. Taken collectively, their impact is tsunami-like. Various kinds of aberrational sexual behavior among consenting adults seem to know no bounds. In each case, new justifications for sexual liaisons outside marriage constitute nothing more nor less than old-fashioned immorality. The judicial branch of the government seems to have nearly unfettered power in terms of redefining relationships, marriage, and the family. The rights of parents with respect to their children are being threatened in an unprecedented manner. The divorce rate continues to rise even as statistics piled upon statistics, accumulated over decades, reveal how paralyzing divorce can be to children and adults alike. Much could be said about each of these factors. Allow, however, a focus on four other developments currently escalating in our society that have impact on the definition and protection of the family.

Number One: An alarming number of adults are unmarried. U.S. Census Bureau numbers reveal that married-couple households—which since the founding of this country have dominated our society—have slipped from nearly 80 percent in the 1950s to just 50 percent today.

A recent cover story in a major news magazine addressed the topic as follows: "Today's culture may be so marriage-crazed . . . precisely because the rite is so threatened. Indeed, we are delaying marriage longer than ever, cohabitating in greater numbers, forming more same-sex partnerships, living far longer, and remarrying less after we split up. What many once thought of as the fringe is becoming the new normal. Families consisting of bread-winner dads and stay-at-home moms now account for just one-tenth of all households. Married couples with kids, which made up nearly every residence a century ago, now total just 25 percent—with the number projected to drop to 20% by 2010, says the Census Bureau. By then, nearly 30% of homes will be inhabited by someone who lives alone" ("Unmarried America," *Business Week,* 20 October 2003, 106–16).

This article painted a picture of what happens nightly in most cities around the world, as highlighted by a depiction of a young adult woman's repeated forays looking for male prospects:

"Most Thursday nights, Hilary Herskowitz slips on her Seven jeans, chooses from among her dozens of shoes, and steps out for an evening . . . with the modish throngs of Manhattan. The 35-year-old communications director and her designer-clad wing girls—a pediatrician, a health-care manager, and an executive recruiter—cruise the city's swankiest bashes: the posh private parties, the paparazzi-stalked soirees. They don't just watch *Sex in the City,* they live it. But after 13 years of this behind-the-velvet-ropes scene, they have yet to find the one thing they want most: husbands. . . . Thirty years ago a single woman like Herskowitz would have been considered an aberration. An old maid. Today, she is so typical that the highest IQs in Hollywood and on Wall Street and Madison Avenue are fixated on dreaming up products for the swelling ranks of unattached urbanites just like her."

The article concluded with this chilling statement: "Fully 54% of female high school seniors say they believe that having a child outside of marriage is a worthwhile lifestyle, up from 33% in 1980, according to the University of Michigan Survey Research Center. And 40% of female twentysomethings would consider having a baby on their own if they reached their mid-30s and hadn't found the right man to marry. What was once a frowned-upon alternative has become the mainstream. Since 1970, the ranks of the never-married and childless have surged astronomically, according to the Census Bureau. There is also a creeping disconnect between marriage and child-rearing with an 850% increase since 1960 in the number of unmarried couples living with kids" (ibid.).

In short, a major issue affecting the family is not only the tremendous increase in the number of unmarried single adults, but the fact that living as an adult in something other than a traditional marriage is now considered socially acceptable, and in some circles even preferred. Most problematic, being single has been made to appear normal—which is a great satanic ploy. Because again, it Lucifer can make an aberration seem normal—or better yet, *evil* seem normal—he has made striking inroads.

Speaking from decades of experience as a single adult, I can say unequivocally that being single is *not* normal. Yes, single adults who have not yet had the privilege of marrying have no choice but to move on with their lives when marriage doesn't occur. They can find countless opportunities to grow and serve and contribute—but even the joys and rewards that can accompany personal progression and selfless service never diminish the sense of loneliness and incompleteness inherent within singleness. There is simply no adequate compensation for not being married, and that is as it should be. For, as the Lord taught Adam, it is "not good that the man should be alone; wherefore [He made] an help meet for him" (Moses 3:18).

> *There is simply no adequate compensation for not being married, and that is as it should be. For, as the Lord taught Adam, it is "not good that the man should be alone."*

Number Two: There has been a phenomenal escalation in, proliferation of, and access to pornography—for both men and women, boys and girls. Statistics documenting this plague—a scourge to rival anything Moses and the children of Israel ever dealt with—paint a sordid story. Here are just a few:

- The word *sex* is the number-one topic searched online
- 90 percent of all seventeen-year-olds have viewed pornography online
- 25 percent of all websites are porn sites, which are estimated at roughly half a million sites
- The worldwide revenue for pornography is $57 billion, or more than the combined revenue of ABC, CBS, and NBC

(As cited in *Ensign,* November 2004, 61)

To put this social and moral blight in further perspective, a recent survey of 443 wards from Provo to Brigham City, Utah, indicated that 68 percent of young LDS men have been exposed to pornography. In some wards it was 100 percent.

President Gordon B. Hinckley has warned in the plainest terms against the corrosive influence of pornography, acknowledging that "this is a very serious problem even among us" (*Ensign,* November 2004, 61). And Elder Dallin H. Oaks did similarly in the April 2005 general conference, declaring that patrons of porn forfeit the power of their priesthood, lose the companionship of the Spirit, and wound and sometimes destroy their most precious relationships (see *Ensign,* May 2005, 87–90).

Pornography distorts and usually obliterates righteous attitudes about marriage, families, and intimacy. It plays havoc with attitudes about women and undermines every-thing sacred and beautiful about womanhood and woman's divine nature. It decimates marriages and families. And in many instances, pornography leads to fornication and adul-tery, as its patrons—like fish dangling on a hook—ultimately can't resist acting out what they see in print or on screen. Many experts believe pornography to be more addictive than cocaine and other hard narcotics, calling it a particularly difficult addiction to reverse.

I have personally seen the effects of pornography on men, women, and families, and can say from firsthand observation that it wrecks relationships and devastates the children who are subjected to the resulting behavior of their parents. It would be impossible to calculate the number of marriages, and thus families, that have been destroyed because a man's or a woman's addiction to pornography led them to violate marriage vows.

Number Three: We live in a culture where celebrities and their misdeeds are not only tolerated but in some instances trumpeted. Just for a moment, contemplate the accusations and charges—ranging from repeated adultery to child molesta-tion to rape to illegal use of performance-enhancing drugs—that swirl around the rich and famous. It seems we have reached a point where the more bizarre the behavior, the better. For too many are entertained if not titillated by celebrity misbehavior.

Our actions as the public suggest that we don't care. We reelect these people. We continue to buy their DVDs and CDs or tickets to watch them play ball or compete in world-class events. Our children wear their jerseys, hang their posters on the wall, listen to their music, and line up to see their films, reinforcing anew that we consider celebrities' behavior irrelevant as long as we like what they deliver—be it points, movies, votes, or wins.

Several years ago a popular, world-class athlete was diagnosed as being HIV-positive. One of the stories covering that development was fascinating. A leading news magazine featured him on the cover with the bold headline, "Even Me." The article went on to identify his sexual exploits and his response to his affliction, which said, in essence, "Imagine, HIV infection could even happen to someone as rich and famous and popular as I am." Such a mind-set is nothing short of ridiculous, and yet it seems to be indicative of the attitude infiltrating our society at an escalating rate. What an alarming message to send our children and teenagers about marriage, the family, and morality!

Jehovah thundered from Sinai that we were to have no other gods before Him, for he was a jealous God (see Exodus 34:14). Both Nebuchadnezzar and his son Belshazzar lost their kingdoms because they "praised the gods of silver, and gold, of brass, iron, wood, and stone, which see not, nor hear, nor know," while failing to glorify "the God in whose hand thy breath is" (Daniel 5:23).

Nephi, on the other hand, refused to put his "trust in the arm of flesh," knowing that "cursed is he that putteth his trust in the arm of flesh" (2 Nephi 4:34).

Hero worship of celebrities—and in far too many instances, celebrities who routinely violate the commandments of God—is a sign of a sick society. For if we can't and don't expect respectable behavior of those who lead and inspire us, will we in time stop expecting respectable, moral behavior of ourselves?

We place ourselves in grave danger when we worship actors, athletes, politicians, and others of notoriety. For the arm of flesh will always, ultimately, let us down.

Number Four: Gay marriage has become socially acceptable and is even legal in some areas. It is difficult to even approach this topic for fear of arousing deep emotion, and yet ignoring this issue that has such direct bearing on the traditional family would be a bit like pretending there isn't an elephant in the middle of the room—when there is one.

I do not pretend to understand same-sex attraction. I don't understand why it occurs. I don't understand what same-sex inclinations feel like. I do, however, have a number of friends who grapple with same-gender attraction. Some of them are living an openly gay lifestyle; others are not acting on their inclinations. Some of those living an openly gay lifestyle have adopted children. They love their children, and their children love them. When a dear and longtime friend of mine died of AIDS recently, I was heartsick. He and I had had many long talks about his choice of lifestyle, and though we did not see things at all the same, I nonetheless cared about him dearly.

I love these friends, every one of them, and they know I love them. In many cases, we have had long, animated conversations about the issue of same-gender attraction. And we've had rigorous debates about gay marriage. I have tried to hear what they've had to say, and they have given me the courtesy of hearing my point of view. After all the dialogue, I don't agree with them, and they don't agree with me. They know, however, that although I have strong feelings about this issue, I do not feel it's my prerogative to judge them for their choices, just as I hope they won't judge me for mine. Their choices are between them and God, just as my choices are. We fought an intense premortal battle for the right to choose, and I would defend their right to live how and with whom they choose.

And one more thing: Those who deal with same-gender attraction, who do *not* respond to those inclinations, and who, in fact, make and honor sacred covenants, have my deepest respect.

Although I would defend the right of those with same-gender attraction to live as they choose, however, I can never defend the proposition that a relationship between two men or two women should be equated with a loving relationship between a man and a woman who marry. That is because I cannot betray or trifle with a law of God. A law that calls for complete abstinence from sexual relations before marriage and total fidelity within marriage. A law decreeing that sexual relations are to be deployed and enjoyed only by a man and a woman legally and lawfully married. A law that, as we learn in the temple, we must obey in order to have any hope of receiving celestial glory. This law? It is the law of chastity.

Our Father is the one who defined and set the pattern for marriage, and any attempt to redefine this pattern is simply not something covenant-making men and women can support. Our Father did not send two men or two women into the Garden. He placed Adam and Eve in the Garden and said, "Be fruitful, and multiply, and replenish the earth" (Moses 2:28), thus delineating the order of things as well as the highest priority of a husband and wife—to procreate. In that moment, our Father established the divine pattern for men and women, marriage and families.

He set the pattern and the circumstances under which the privilege of sexual intimacy is to be enjoyed.

The First Presidency and Council of the Twelve Apostles reconfirmed that pattern in "The Family: A Proclamation to the World": "Marriage between a man and a woman is ordained of God. . . . God's commandment for His children to multiply and replenish the earth remains in force. . . . The sacred powers of procreation are to be employed only between man and woman, lawfully wedded as husband and wife."

They further explained just how seriously God views any trifling with this law: "We warn that individuals who violate the covenants of chastity, who abuse spouse or offspring, or who fail to fulfill family responsibilities will one day stand accountable before God. Further, we warn that the disintegration of the family will bring upon individuals, communities, and nations the calamities foretold by ancient and modern prophets" (*Ensign*, November 1995, 102).

In short, there is *no* relationship—not between two men or two women, not between colleagues or teammates or siblings or the dearest of friends—that compares with that of a man and a woman who commit to and covenant with each other in marriage, who remain faithful to each other, and who co-create a family unit.

Said President Gordon B. Hinckley: "God-sanctioned

marriage between a man and a woman has been the basis of civilization for thousands of years. There is no justification to redefine what marriage is. Such is not our right, and those who try will find themselves answerable to God.

"Some portray legalization of so-called same-sex marriage as a civil right. This is not a matter of civil rights; it is a matter of morality. . . . Our hearts reach out to those who refer to themselves as gays and lesbians. We love and honor them as sons and daughters of God. They are welcome in the Church. It is expected, however, that they follow the same God-given rules of conduct that apply to everyone else, whether single or married" (*Ensign*, November 1999, 54).

Some form of immorality lies at the root of most of the problems that undermine, threaten, or destroy families.

The law of chastity is a law of God. And it applies equally to everyone, regardless of circumstances, marital status, or sexual attraction.

This brief overview of just four of many factors affecting the definition and institution of marriage and the family reveals an undeniable theme: that Satan's dominant strategy against marriage and the family is to inspire and promote immorality—or violations of the law of chastity. Indeed, almost all of Lucifer's attacks against the family today are morally based. Why does he try the same old tactics again and again? Because, sadly, they work again and again, even among Latter-day Saints.

It would be impossible to calculate the damage done and lives almost irreparably altered by some sort of moral violation. Consider the arsenal of weapons Lucifer uses: sexual abuse, pornography, adultery, unwed pregnancy, homosexuality and gay marriage, blatant promiscuity, abortion—and the list goes on and on. The stunning bottom line? Some form of immorality lies at the root of most of the problems that undermine, threaten, or destroy families—either immorality that someone chooses to participate in, or immorality that affects the innocent.

In short and in essence, the law of chastity defines the family.

A professor of marriage and family therapy at Brigham Young University who has taught graduate students and worked as a marriage and family therapist for more than thirty years was recently asked how many couples she had counseled directly or supervised the counseling of during those years. She estimated to have worked with well over five thousand—75 percent of whom were LDS. She was then asked what percentage of those couples came to her because of distress in their lives that did *not* have any kind of immorality (meaning anything from abuse to pornography to adultery) as the root cause of the issue. Her response? "Less than 10 percent."

Her experience may be atypical. But on the other hand, it might not be. And as sobering as her response was, perhaps it shouldn't surprise us, for the forces of evil will do anything and everything imaginable to destroy marriages and families. It is one of Satan's quickest and most effective ways of attempting to thwart the plan of salvation. Further, it is his way of interfering with an institution destined to

> *The adversary loves to represent the law of chastity as a law of denial, which is a devastating lie. The law of chastity is actually a grand key to spiritual progression.*

survive forever, as Elder Neal A. Maxwell explained: "When the surf of the centuries has made the great pyramids so much sand, the everlasting family will still be standing, because it is a celestial institution, formed outside telestial time" (*Ensign,* May 1978, 10–11).

Consider, just as an example, the tactic Lucifer has vigorously championed on the issue of abortion, which is one way he has attempted to keep spirits from receiving bodies and entering their mortal estate. He has managed to position abortion as a principle of choice. "Shouldn't a woman have the right to choose if she does or does not have a baby?" shout the pro-abortion advocates. The response we seldom hear is that, yes, while a woman should have her agency to choose if she wishes to have a baby, once the baby has been conceived, the choice has been made. It's a farce to believe that Satan would support anything that gives any of Heavenly Father's children a choice.

The forces of evil actively promote gross distortions of sexual intimacy—the more bizarre the relationship or relationships, the better—and rejoice every time a child is conceived out of wedlock and therefore out of the covenant and outside the protection of the holy priesthood. Immorality of any kind keeps men and women from entering into the new and everlasting covenant of marriage and thus keeps them also outside the protection of the priesthood and the Holy Ghost.

Pornography creates an entirely false impression of love, intimacy, and marriage, all while presenting a distorted view of women and womanhood. Homosexuality thwarts procreation and spiritual progression. And again, all of these keep men, women, and children outside the protection of the priesthood and the Holy Ghost.

The adversary loves to represent the law of chastity as a

law of denial, which is a disgusting, devastating lie. The law of chastity is actually a grand key to spiritual progression and to gaining greater spiritual power. And Satan knows it, which is why his attacks are so relentless and deadly. For when a marriage is sealed in the house of the Lord, a man and woman can draw upon more godly power than is available in any other relationship, as was revealed to the Prophet Joseph Smith: "If a man marry a wife by my word, which is my law, and by the new and everlasting covenant, and it is sealed unto them by the Holy Spirit of promise, . . . [they shall] inherit thrones, kingdoms, principalities, and powers, dominions, all heights and depths—. . . and they shall pass by the angels, and the gods, which are set there, to their exaltation and glory in all things, as hath been sealed upon their heads, which glory shall be a fulness and a continuation of the seeds forever and ever. Then shall they be gods, because they have no end. . . . Then shall they be gods, because they have all power, and the angels are subject unto them" (D&C 132:19, 20).

Thus, if men and women are to realize their full potential and become gods, they must enter into the new and everlasting covenant of marriage—which covenant is available only to those worthy to enter the house of the Lord and be sealed as companions for time and all eternity.

On the other hand, every time physical intimacy is

abused, it decreases a man or woman's access to godly power. It destroys spirituality and perverts what the Lord intended to be a sacramental kind of experience between husband and wife that can bring them closer to each other and to the Lord.

Consider for a moment the spiritual privileges a couple forfeit when they indulge in immorality:

They cannot enter the temple, so they cannot receive the highest ordinances of the Melchizedek Priesthood or a fulness of the Holy Ghost. Neither can their marriage be sealed by the Holy Spirit of Promise. They therefore forgo the opportunity of an eternal family or eternal increase, the ramifications of which are devastating. Properly used, the gift of procreation—and it is a gift—will eventually result in endless increase, or the ability to eternally procreate spirit sons and daughters, which is one of the major characteristics that makes God who He is—*God the Father!* Our Father. Those who abuse the gift forfeit that eternal blessing.

Those who violate the law of chastity also cut themselves off from personal revelation and from communion with the Father and the Son, for "the Spirit of the Lord doth not dwell in unholy temples" (Helaman 4:24). With repeated violations, the Lord eventually withdraws His protective and matchless power.

They are not able to partake of the sacrament—at least

worthily—and therefore distance themselves from the redemptive and enabling power of Jesus Christ. Thus they place themselves in a position where they are unlikely to be able to access godly power.

And, most remarkably, they give up the opportunity for exaltation.

Those who violate the law of chastity in essence trade the most glorious privileges God has offered His children for brief encounters that leave them ultimately unfulfilled and spiritually devastated.

Living the law of chastity is the linchpin to every significant spiritual privilege. It is the gateway to immortality.

One of this life's greatest ironies is that those who partake unworthily of sexual intimacy, and wish to do so forever, won't be able to. Orson Pratt explained that "when the sons and daughters of the Most High God come forth in the morning of the resurrection, this principle of love will exist in their bosoms just as it exists here, only intensified according to the increased knowledge and understanding which they possess; hence, they will be capacitated to enjoy the relationship of husband and wife . . . in a hundred fold degree greater than they could in mortality" (*Journal of Discourses*, 13:187).

Is it worth it to be pure, to conceive of enjoying a relationship that is a hundred times sweeter and deeper than anything mortality has to offer? Further, even in mortality, a pure relationship between a husband and wife—meaning one enjoyed within the bonds of marriage—is ten thousand times sweeter than one tainted with guilt, regret, mistrust, and deceit. Ask any priesthood leader, any marriage and family therapist, or, for that matter, anyone who has violated the law of chastity and then walked the long and painful road back, and they'll testify that Orson Pratt's comment applies to this life as well as to the next. No suggestive DVD, movie, or song lyric can come close to capturing the sweet feelings that flow between a man and a woman who have made sacred covenants with each other and who become one as the Lord intended.

Very simply, living the law of chastity is the linchpin to every significant spiritual privilege. Living the law of chastity is the gateway to immortality.

The Family Proclamation is clear about the virtue of virtue, as well as the impact of virtue on marriage and family: "The family is ordained of God. Marriage between man and woman is essential to His eternal plan. Children are entitled to birth within the bonds of matrimony, and to be reared by a father and a mother who honor marital vows with complete fidelity. Happiness in family life is most likely to be achieved when founded upon the teachings of the Lord Jesus Christ."

Imagine what would happen to couples and families throughout the entire world, and therefore what would happen to the world, if men and women everywhere simply understood and embraced these simple truths: that happiness in family life is linked to living the gospel of Jesus Christ. And that the law of chastity is the law that defines the family as God intended it to be.

The law of chastity defines the family as our Father intended it to be defined. It is not a law of denial but a law of supernal power and joy. It is a law that brings with its observance glorious eternal promises.

Chapter Six

Purity Gives Women Power

Twenty-one years of service in various Relief Society presidencies has introduced me to women around the world and blessed me with vivid images of them and their lives. I can picture a twenty-one-year-old district Relief Society president in Phnom Penh, riding to meetings on the back of a moped; women who make living in the heat of the Amazon look easy; women in Siberia who recognized truth in spite of the fact that they had never even heard of Jesus Christ. Again and again, I have seen dramatic evidence of the influence of women—beginning with mothers but including also grandmothers, aunts, and sisters—in building and maintaining strong families.

Here is what I've come to believe: that women have unusual power to strengthen and build families. But they also have unusual power to destroy them.

I've never been able to find the words to adequately articulate the depth and breadth of a righteous woman's reach. It is simply not possible to measure or limit the influence a righteous woman has on her husband and children and extended family members, as well as on others who feel like family.

Women have unusual power to strengthen and build families. But they also have unusual power to destroy them.

But evil women are scary. In some respects, they are scarier than evil men, because in order for Satan to obtain a secure grasp on a woman, he must first completely neutralize her nature, including her divine gifts. It would be impossible to calculate the number of men, young and old, who have fallen for traps laid by seductive women they couldn't resist.

A scene from Shakespeare's *Macbeth* depicts the chilling consequences of a woman's forsaking her nature. As Lady Macbeth tries to persuade her husband to murder the king and seize his throne, she taunts him: "Thy nature [is] too full o' the milk of human kindness"—meaning, he's too much like a woman. Then later from her balcony she petitions the source of evil to "unsex me here" and "fill me . . . with direst cruelty. . . . Take my [woman's] milk for gall. . . . Come, thick night!" (*Macbeth*, Act I, scene 5.) In other words, she realizes that she must completely repudiate her divine gifts as a woman if she is to take a human life.

Women who have surrendered their divine nature to Satan are both frightening and pathetic, for their situation represents a dire reversal of the gifts our Father gave His daughters premortally. He endowed women with the nature to nurture and the inclination to bless and heal, encourage and inspire.

But Satan has done everything he can to confuse all of society about women, and to confuse women about themselves. As just one example, in July 2005, a prominent national magazine released its listing of the world's 100 Most Powerful Women. Almost every woman on the list—*every one*—was included because of her political, business, or entertainment prominence. Motherhood was almost entirely ignored or at the very least devalued. It is ironic that, on a list purportedly developed to champion the achievements of those women deemed most accomplished in the world's eyes, the work that most women in the history of the world have performed and continue to perform was overlooked. The very listing itself actually undermines women in general (see *Forbes*, July 2005).

President J. Reuben Clark Jr. declared motherhood to be "as divinely called and as eternally important in its place as the Priesthood itself" (*Relief Society Magazine*, December 1946, 801). More recently, Elder Jeffrey R. Holland put motherhood in historical as well as spiritual perspective: Mothers, "Yours is the grand tradition of Eve, the mother of all the human family. . . . Yours is the grand tradition of Sarah and Rebekah and Rachel, without whom there could not have been those magnificent patriarchal promises to Abraham, Isaac, and Jacob. . . . Yours is the grand tradition of Lois and Eunice and the mothers of the 2,000 stripling warriors. Yours is the grand tradition of Mary, chosen and foreordained from before this world was, to conceive, carry, and bear the Son of God Himself. We thank all of you . . . and tell you there is nothing more important in this world than participating so directly in the work and glory of God. . . . Yours is the work of salvation, and therefore you will be magnified, compensated, made more than you are and better than you have ever been as you try to make an honest effort, however feeble you may sometimes feel that to be" (*Ensign,* May 1997, 36).

President Hinckley recently remarked, as he has so many times before, that the credit for raising five faithful, accomplished children goes to his wife, Marjorie. When asked to describe the essence of her mothering, he responded simply, "She helped our children feel well about themselves." Women—and particularly women of God who have the Holy Ghost with them and are filled with the pure love of Christ—have an endless and eternal impact on those they love, especially their children. As far as I'm concerned, such an impact far exceeds any contribution a woman makes leading a company or even a nation. It's not that there isn't value in those pursuits; the point here is not about value or comparisons, but about perspective and priorities. What can possibly equate with nurturing and shaping a human life?

Elder Neal A. Maxwell put the contribution of mothers in perspective when he said, "When the real history of mankind is fully disclosed, will it feature the echoes of gunfire or the shaping sound of lullabies? The great armistices made by military men or the peacemaking of women in homes and in neighborhoods? Will what happened in cradles and kitchens prove to be more controlling than what happened in congresses?" (*Ensign*, May 1978, 10–11).

It is no wonder that Satan has declared war on mother-hood. He understands full well that those who rock the cradle can rock his earthly empire, or Babylon. And he knows that without righteous mothers loving and leading the next generation, the kingdom of God will fail. When we understand—when we even catch a glimpse—of the magnitude of motherhood as God intended it to be, it becomes clear why prophets have been so protective of a woman's most sacred role.

Women are uniquely positioned to teach and model virtue and the law of chastity.

President Joseph F. Smith taught that women, and par-ticularly mothers, have such profound influence because "the love of a true mother comes nearer to being like the love of God than any other kind of love" (*Improvement Era*, May 1913, 730). And President Boyd K. Packer elaborated even further on the extent of a righteous woman's influ-ence: "However much priesthood power and authority the men may possess . . . the safety of the family, the integrity of the doctrine, the ordinances, the covenants, indeed the future of the Church, rests equally upon the women" (*Ensign*, May 1998, 73).

Mothers and grandmothers, sisters and favorite aunts and Primary teachers—indeed, women in every station of life—are uniquely positioned to teach and model virtue and the law of chastity, and to model how to stand up for both with courage and poise.

On the other hand, if a woman chooses to use her power and influence unrighteously, the effects can be devastating. One has to wonder if a major reason our society is experiencing such a steep moral slide is because of the dramatic increase in the number of women tampering with or violating the law of chastity. Prime-time TV shows such as *Desperate Housewives* and *Sex in the City* would have horrified viewers just a few years ago, but today they seem to indicate a remarkable tolerance—even an unbelievable degree of encouragement—for the sexual misbehavior of women, including married women. Further, the messages such programs communicate about womanhood are utterly erroneous and completely misrepresent our Father's view of His daughters.

In a magnificent address entitled "The Moral Influence of Women" delivered at the World Congress on the Family in 1999, Elder Bruce C. Hafen declared that throughout history women have tended to be society's primary teachers and guardians of sexual and moral values. He quoted Leon Kass as saying this: "A fine woman understood that giving her body, even her kiss, meant giving her heart, which was too precious to be bestowed on anyone who would not prove himself worthy, at the very least, by pledging himself in marriage to be her defender and her lover forever." Thus, "it is largely through the purity of her morals, self-regulated, that woman wields her influence. Men will always do what is pleasing to women, but only if women suitably control and channel their own considerable sexual power" ("The End of Courtship," *The Public Interest,* Winter 1997, 39).

Over the centuries, a majority of women have responded to men's inappropriate advances with, "No, not until marriage." That must be at least part of the reason the Lord "delight[s] in the chastity of women" (Jacob 2:28). But tragically, this trend appears to be shifting.

Recently the bishop of a young single adult ward confirmed for me what several other bishops presiding over singles' wards have acknowledged. "I am dealing more with promiscuity and immorality among the young adult women in my ward than I am with the young men," this concerned bishop lamented. "Most of the young men are returned missionaries and have made covenants in the temple to be chaste, and that seems to help them, but far too many of my young women are succumbing to sexual advances, often in an effort to overcome their feelings of low self-worth. Ironically, even moments after intimacy, they feel more worthless than ever before."

At least part of the cause for this appears to be an erosion of female attitudes about sacred things, beginning with their bodies. Immodesty in American society and even among our own people has reached epidemic proportions. Particularly during summer months, an increasing percentage of women attend church and partake of sacred ordinances—including in the temple—in what could only be considered beach or picnic attire. While young men who are handling the emblems of the sacrament typically attend sacrament meeting dressed in white shirts and ties, young women (and too often their mothers) arrive wearing tight, second-skin clothing and flip-flops.

Perhaps the problem is that we haven't stopped to think about what actually happens, for example, in sacrament meeting. The chapel is regarded and treated differently from any other room in a meetinghouse because it is an ordinance room—the room where we present ourselves before the Lord to renew our covenants with Him and then to partake of the sacrament, an ordinance. The operative question should be: If we were to have a personal interview with the Savior, what would we wear? In sacrament meeting, we are, in effect, meeting individually with the Lord to make an accounting of the previous week and to renew our promise to follow Him.

When we enter the temple, we actually enter the house of the Lord as invited guests, therein to partake of sacred ordinances that allow us to draw upon the power of God. Again, clothing befitting that privilege is in order.

Unfortunately, a walk through any airport or mall, a glance through any magazine on any news rack, will show women wearing clothing that can only be classified as underwear—clothing that we as latter-day women and daughters of God are attempting to duplicate far too often as our society becomes increasingly, alarmingly casual. Some of our clothing is too tight, too short, too low-cut, too suggestive, too revealing. Then we wonder why our teenage sons struggle to remain chaste in thought and deed, or, for that matter, why some of our forty-nine-year-old men struggle in the same way.

Elder Dallin H. Oaks sounded this warning to women: "Please understand that if you dress immodestly, you are magnifying this problem by becoming pornography to some of the men who see you" (*Ensign*, May 2005, 90). Women of God who understand what it means to be God's offspring saved for the latter days dare not risk looking like the women of the world, some of whom increasingly look like harlots. Are we beginning to sound too much, look too much, and act too much like the women of the world?

Bottom line? Women are ideally suited to model and teach modesty and the law of chastity. But they are also ideally positioned to erode the law of chastity and to make modesty a virtue from a bygone era. And this trend is escalating at unprecedented speed.

How, then, do covenant-making men and women respond? How do we fight back by standing up for what we know to be true?

First, we need to realize what is happening all around us that affects our view and understanding of men and women, marriage, and the family. We also need to find every meaningful way within our sphere of influence to teach our Father's plan for His children, including His plan for families. And that includes helping teach correct views about men, women, and their relationships with one another.

Second, in the case of women, motherhood needs to be re-enshrined. An article in a recent national publication caught my attention. A woman described taking a recent international trip where, instead of photographing famous landmarks along the way, she had found herself photographing mothers with their children. She wrote, "After I returned home and had the pictures developed, I . . . kept looking at them. Especially at the children. They were so utterly sweet, so utterly small. I felt a pain in my chest; I was as sad and bereft as I have ever been in my life. It was at that moment I began grieving that I had never had children of my own" (*Ladies' Home Journal*, August 2005, 72).

I am now fifty-one and have not yet had the privilege of marrying—not by choice, I hasten to add. And therefore I have not been blessed with the privilege of bearing children. Though I have had countless stretching, life-changing opportunities and experiences, I nonetheless feel a deep sense of loss because I have missed out on the single most meaningful experience a woman can have—that of bearing children. What could possibly be more important or enduring than bringing a life into the world and then shepherding that life so that he or she can fulfill a God-given, divine potential? All I can say is that no other success or contribution or experience equates or compensates.

The Prophet Joseph is reported to have said that "the time would come when none but the women of the Latter-day Saints would be willing to bear children" (*Young Woman's Journal* 2 [10 September 1890]: 81). And

Lorenzo Snow declared that "a mother who has brought up a family of faithful children ought to be saved, if she never does another good thing" (*Improvement Era*, 22:651).

The light the gospel shines on the divine role of women and motherhood is something the entire world needs to see. And sometimes, the response of the world to true principles can be surprising.

In the spring of 2003 I was unexpectedly appointed as a White House delegate to the Commission on the Status of Women at the United Nations, which proved to be an entirely foreign experience in every way. It had its own "language," its own set of rules—everything. As a result of that appointment to serve, I was subsequently invited to attend a world policy forum on the family held at BYU. The attendees included a host of policymakers, including many ambassadors and U.N. heads of delegation from around the world—all of whom were devoted to defending and protecting the family.

At the conclusion of the first day of the three-day event, one of the conference organizers approached me and asked if I could help them with a problem that had just developed. A General Authority had been scheduled to speak at their concluding dinner, but he had suddenly been called out of town. "We need a speaker, and we need it to be you," they said, dropping the proverbial bomb.

I vigorously protested that for obvious reasons—meaning, my marital status—I couldn't possibly be the best choice to speak to that group, but in the end I agreed and then spent two days agonizing over what to say to such a culturally and religiously diverse audience. I couldn't think of anything I could say about sensitive, family-related issues that wouldn't offend someone there.

As I drove to the dinner that evening, I was still unsure about what to say. But when the time came for me to address the group, I found myself articulating a message far different from the one I had anticipated giving. "I was introduced as a member of The Church of Jesus Christ of Latter-day Saints," I began, "and as members of our Church, my parents taught me from childhood about the importance of marriage and the family. They also taught me to live the law of chastity, which I came to understand meant abstinence from all sexual relations before marriage and complete fidelity within marriage.

"There came a time in my life when I adopted the beliefs of my parents and made a promise to God that I would indeed live this law," I continued. "I am about to turn fifty years old, and I have not yet married, but I have been faithful to the promise I made to God."

I then went on to acknowledge that, despite the obvious challenges, I felt on the whole that this choice had actually proven to be easier than the alternative. I explained that although I'd had plenty of lonely days and nights, I had never had a moment's worry over an abortion, an unwanted pregnancy, or a sexually transmitted disease. I hadn't had to deal with the feelings of being used and then abandoned by a man. I'd never spent one second regretting violating a promise to God, because I had not violated that promise. "So," I concluded, "I must tell you that I believe a moral life is actually an easier, more wonderful life."

I then acknowledged the pain we as a family had experienced due to the untimely death of my brother, who left a wife and three young children behind, and, later, an accident that took the lives of a young niece and nephew. But I explained that I had never seen more pain than I had earlier that year when I was present as a father and mother told their children they were separating as a result of the father's immorality.

I concluded with a plea: "You are men and women of influence. For three days you have articulated the problems attacking families, most of which have a moral, or immoral, root. I plead with you to speak more openly about the need for chastity, because if more men and women would live the law of chastity, it would change the world."

To my utter astonishment, before I could get back to my table, the people in the audience were on their feet applauding. That clearly had nothing to do with me personally. It happened simply because they recognized truth when it was taught. Most interestingly, one woman after another, from disparate cultures and continents, sought me out afterwards. Every one of them said essentially the same thing: "I wish I'd heard you give this message when I was young. It would have changed my life."

I can think of few things that would do more to build stronger families than to teach and model the law of chastity. And perhaps there are few things that would do more good in today's world than for virtue-loving, covenant-keeping women to stand up, speak up, and live up to their values and beliefs. We are uniquely positioned to teach by word and deed that purity actually diminishes Satan's ability to influence us, and that virtue is the key to happiness, while immorality always results in pain and sorrow. I have yet to meet the man or woman who is happier because he or she has committed adultery.

As one who has faced the challenge of living a completely chaste life and of living alone far longer than I would have ever imagined or hoped, I can testify that the law of chastity was instituted by our Father and endorsed by His Son. Observing this law results in happiness and peace of mind. There is power, spiritual power, in increased purity. There is power in living the law of chastity, which is a law from God.

Chapter Seven

You May Be Making Life Harder Than It Needs to Be

The company for which I work is constantly conducting research to find out how customers feel about everything from our retail stores to the products on our shelves to the subjects they wish our authors would address. A recent research project focusing on the needs and concerns of women was instituted to help our publishing division in their brainstorming regarding new products. One question invited the women surveyed to identify the top three things they cared deeply about but felt they weren't handling very well. Far and away the most common response from more than 200 women was this: They cared greatly about feeling close to the Lord and increasing their spirituality, but didn't feel they were making much progress in that regard. A subsequent question asked the women to explain why they felt they weren't doing well. The list of responses was uncanny, because all 200 were essentially the same. The answers read generally like this: "I know I should pray more, and I know I should read the scriptures, but I get caught up in everyday life and don't do it. I know those things would make a difference."

It's curious. We want to be close to our Father and His Son, but often we don't do the very things—some of them so simple and straightforward that we teach our Primary children how to do them—that will help us draw down the powers of heaven into our lives.

The first chapter of this book focused on the reality that life was not meant to be a picnic, and that if it were, it would lose all power to accelerate our growth toward godhood. The Apostle Paul taught the Romans that "we are the children of God: And if children, then heirs; heirs of God, and joint-heirs with Christ; *if* so be that we suffer with him, that we may be also glorified together" (Romans 8:16–17; emphasis added).

In other words, there is a price to be paid if we wish to reap the ultimate reward of being exalted and inheriting all the Father has. We are children of God, and this mortal experience is a uniquely designed tutorial—adapted individually to each of us—that gives us the opportunity to become joint-heirs with Christ. We can never give what He gave, because it is not within our capacity to do so. But we can give *all we can give,* which constitutes our own great offering and sacrifice. It's the principle of the widow's mite. We give—and in some situations give up—*all* that we can give or give up as we seek to follow the Lord, learn His ways, draw upon His power, and see His face.

The familiar statement of a member of the Martin Handcart Company is revealing: "Was I sorry that I chose to come by handcart? No. Neither then nor any minute of my life since. The price we paid to become acquainted with God was a privilege to pay, and I am thankful that I was privileged to come in the Martin Handcart Company."

In this faithful pioneer's description of the ordeal he and so many others endured, he explained further what "becoming acquainted with God" meant to him: "I have pulled my handcart when I was so weak and weary from illness and lack of food that I could hardly put one foot ahead of the other. I have looked ahead and seen a patch of sand or a hill slope and I have said, I can go only that far and there I must give up. . . . I have gone on to that sand and when I reached it, the cart began pushing me. I have looked back many times to see who was pushing my cart, but my eyes saw no one. I knew then that the angels of God were there" (*Relief Society Magazine*, January 1948, 8).

He described an element of life we may all expect: that we will experience moments and episodes where the intensity of the challenge nearly defeats us. Apparently it was meant to be so. President John Taylor reported hearing the Prophet Joseph say that "you will have all kinds of trials to pass through. And it is quite as necessary for you to be tried as it was for Abraham and other men of God. . . . God will feel after you, and He will take hold of you and wrench your very heart strings, and if you cannot stand it you will not be fit for an inheritance in the Celestial Kingdom of God" (*Journal of Discourses*, 24:197).

If you're serious about sanctification, you can expect to experience heart-wrenching moments that try your faith, your endurance, and your patience.

President Joseph F. Smith addressed the same theme in a slightly different way: "I contend that a man is in a poor condition to endure the trials and temptations in the world who is not tried in his feelings and proven to the uttermost, to see if he loves the truth *more than he loves himself or the world*" (Conference Report, 4 April 1897; emphasis added).

In short, if you're serious about sanctification, you can expect to experience heart-wrenching moments that try your faith, your endurance, and your patience. Where will you turn in the midst of heartache or privation?

Truly, if life were easy, it wouldn't be hard. However, it may be that many of us are making life far more difficult than it needs or is supposed to be. As the handcart pioneer discovered, he was not expected to make his grueling journey alone. He learned firsthand that there was help; there was power available *for him* from beyond the veil.

The same is true for us. We are not alone—at least, we're alone only if we choose to be alone. We're alone only if we choose to go through life relying solely on our own strength rather than learning to draw upon the power of God. Thus, the question for each of us is, what do we believe?

Do we believe there is power in the gospel of Jesus Christ, power in the Atonement, power in the gift of the Holy Ghost, power in the ordinances of the temple, power in the Word to help us, guide us, and strengthen us far beyond any individual gifts we may have? Do we believe the promise the Lord has made countless times, epitomized by this verse: "If thou shalt ask, thou shalt receive *revelation upon revelation, knowledge upon knowledge,* that *thou mayest know the mysteries* and peaceable things—that which bringeth joy, that which bringeth life eternal" (D&C 42:61; emphasis added).

As compelling as those words are, what the Lord did *not* say is perhaps of equal interest. He did not say that if you're the President of the Church, or a stake president, or have been married in the temple, or have raised seven children to serve missions, you may receive these things. He said, "If thou shalt ask," putting the responsibility for seeking the Lord directly on our shoulders and within reach of anyone.

As Nephi declared, "He that diligently seeketh shall find; and the mysteries of God shall be unfolded unto them, by the power of the Holy Ghost, as well in these times as in times of old." He then went on to add that this promise also applied "as well in times of old as in times to come" (1 Nephi 10:19). In other words, the promise holds for us. *Most* personal revelation occurs in response to our pleadings and petitions.

The mysteries of God—meaning, knowledge about His nature and character, and particularly knowledge about how He works—are as available to us today as they were to Adam or Noah or Nephi. Alma taught Zeezrom that "it is given unto *many* to know the mysteries of God" (Alma 12:9; emphasis added). He went on to describe that mysteries are revealed to those who seek the Lord with "heed and diligence," adding this important piece of explanation: "He that will harden his heart, the same receiveth the lesser portion of the word; and he that will not harden his heart, to him is given the greater portion of the word, until it is given unto him to know the mysteries of God *until he know them in full*" (Alma 12:10; emphasis added). The meaning is clear: Those who harden their hearts to their spiritual possibilities receive less; those who believe and open their hearts to God have the potential of learning everything the Lord has written into His divine curriculum.

Moroni spoke of something similar when, after recording a magnificent menu of spiritual gifts available to us all, he taught that every good gift comes from Christ, that He is the same yesterday, today, and forever, and that "these gifts of which I have spoken, which are spiritual, never will be done away, even as long as the world shall stand, *only according to the unbelief of the children of men*" (Moroni 10:19; emphasis added).

I vividly remember seminary lessons in which we talked about unbelievers, almost always picturing them as heartless, faithless, even obstinate and wicked people. But over the years I have wondered if the most sobering kind of unbelief is actually that of faithful members of the Church sitting in sacrament meeting every week—members who don't really believe the Lord will reveal His mind and will and workings to them, and have thus hardened their hearts to their spiritual possibilities, potential, and privileges.

About this, President George Q. Cannon was emphatic: "We find, even among those who have embraced the Gospel, *hearts of unbelief.* How many of you, my brethren and sisters, are seeking for these gifts that God has promised to bestow? How many of you, when you bow before your Heavenly Father in your family circle or in your secret places, contend for these gifts to be bestowed upon you? How many of you ask the Father, in the name of Jesus, to manifest Himself to you through these powers and these gifts? Or do you go along day by day like a door turning on its hinges, without having any feeling on the subject, without exercising any faith whatever; content to be baptized and be members of the Church, and to rest there, thinking that your salvation is secure because you have done this? I say to you, in the name of the Lord . . . that you have need to repent of this. You have need to repent of your hardness of heart, of your indifference, and of your carelessness. There is not that diligence, there is not that faith, there is not that seeking for the power of God that there should be among a people who have received the precious promises we have. . . . I say to you that it is our duty to avail ourselves of the privileges which God has placed within our reach" (*Millennial Star* 56 [1894]: 259–60; emphasis added).

Remember why Joseph Smith was commanded, during his transcendent experience in the Sacred Grove, *not* to join any church? The reason was at least partly because the churches taught "for doctrines the commandments of men, having a form of godliness, but they deny the power thereof" (Joseph Smith–History 1:19). Are any of us, as covenant sons and daughters, in danger of denying God's power because we don't seek it and perhaps aren't entirely sure He'll truly share His power with us?

Not long ago a friend asked if I would help her hunt for a new home. She'd had a discouraging experience surrounding the probability of a new home and was feeling disheartened about the entire process until we came across a house perched on the side of a cliff that had gorgeous views and other appealing features. "Oh, do you think it's possible *this* could be my new home?" she asked with obvious excitement, adding a request: "Can we pray about this, right now? In fact, will you offer the prayer?" I was happy to, and while praying asked that if it did not run counter to the Lord's will, she might be allowed to live in that home . . . or something better.

The "something better" part caught her attention. It had never occurred to her to pray for "something better" than she was imagining or conceiving. Yet none of us would wish to limit or restrain the Lord by the smallness of our vision or hopes or petitions. The Prophet Joseph didn't hesitate to pray in this manner, as he demonstrated at the dinner table one evening. Looking over the food spread before them, he prayed simply, "Lord, we thank Thee for this Johnny cake, and ask Thee to send us something better. Amen." Before the meal was over, a man came to the door, asked if Joseph was home, and, finding that he was, said, "I have brought you some flour and a ham" (John A. Widtsoe, *Joseph Smith—Seeker after Truth*, 353).

Something better, just as Joseph asked. That prompts the question, Is it possible that the Lord has blessings in mind for us—blessings and gifts and revelations so much better and knowledge so much greater than we have yet conceived, but blessings we haven't received because we don't ask. We don't petition. We don't plead. We don't seek to understand His instructions and promptings as relayed by the Holy Ghost with increasing clarity, frequency, and purity. In other words, we are either distracted by the world or derailed by our unbelief and hard hearts, with the result being the same in either case: We don't receive what He has for us because we don't really, consistently, *diligently* seek after Him.

Webster defines the word *diligent* as "steady, earnest, and energetic application," and as "persevering." As an application, "due diligence," as used in a legal sense, refers to an in-depth, careful scrutiny of an issue or an organization or a company prior to making a crucial decision (and particularly an acquisition). In this case, a steady and earnest evaluation is made of an entity or an issue prior to recommending action. *Due diligence.*

The words *diligently, diligence,* and *diligent* appear in the scriptures almost 200 times, with the promise always being that if we diligently seek or study or labor or teach, we will find and learn and grow. Or, as the Lord declared to the Prophet Joseph: "Seek me *diligently* and ye shall find me; ask, and ye shall receive; knock, and it shall be opened unto you" (D&C 88:63; emphasis added). Never does the Lord say, "Seek me perfectly" or "Seek me to a point of exhaustion." He asks simply that we seek after Him diligently— meaning earnestly, steadily, and with some energy—with the promise being that if we do, we will find Him. Indeed, we have been told that "every soul" who forsakes his or her sins, comes unto Christ, calls on His name, obeys His voice, and keeps His commandments can even see His face and know that He truly lives (see D&C 93:1).

Further, on certain occasions the word *heed* is combined with *diligence.* To *heed* means to "pay attention." The combination of diligently seeking after the Lord and paying attention to His tender mercies, His teachings, and His workings in our lives appears to pay remarkable dividends.

The pointers on the Liahona worked according to the heed and diligence Lehi's family gave them (see 1 Nephi 16:28; Mosiah 1:16); Alma explained that the Lord revealed many mysteries to those who paid heed and diligence to the Word (see Alma 12:9); the people of Nephi and the Church enjoyed great prosperity during the days of Helaman because of the heed and diligence they gave the Word (see Alma 49:30). Heed and diligence—paying attention and earnestly, steadily pursuing to understand the doctrine and to communicate with the Spirit—will ultimately open the heavens. Further, paying attention and earnestly, steadily seeking after the Lord is doable for *anyone* who truly desires to do it.

I know a great woman who has raised a house full of superb children and who with her husband has served long and faithfully in an area where they have been instrumental to the Church's stability and growth. She epitomizes a latter-day woman of God. Not long ago, however, she chided her sister for petitioning the Lord for help on matters "so insignificant," as she described them, as being able to feel rested after just a few hours of sleep or having help with losing weight. "You abuse the Lord," she accused her sister. "You're asking the Lord for something you should do on your own. You shouldn't ask the Lord to bail you out on insignificant things that you should handle yourself."

What this woman didn't understand was that her sister offered those prayers *after* feeling she had cheerfully and consistently done all things in her power but was still in need of extra help from above. She needed the arm of the Lord to be revealed in her behalf (see D&C 123:17). When it comes right down to it, this good woman—a woman who is a true follower of Christ and has devoted her life to building His kingdom—is hesitant to ask or seek or expect too much from the Lord. She doesn't want to bother Him. She believes she should approach the Lord only with huge, life-changing, or life-threatening issues. She doesn't realize that the Lord has more to give her now than she ever imagined—something far better than what she routinely asks for.

Is anything too insignificant to discuss with the Lord? Is any heartache too petty? Is any anxiety or worry too trivial? Is any weakness too insignificant to deal with? The Lord doesn't seem to think so. He has invited us to weary Him with our requests and needs. He has counseled us to pray over our flocks and fields, to cry unto Him for all of His support, to counsel with Him in *all* our doings so that He can direct us for good, to pour out our souls in our closets and in our wilderness, to have our "hearts be full, drawn out in prayer unto him *continually* for [our] welfare" (Alma 34:27, emphasis added; see also Alma 34:18–26; 37:36–37). "All our doings" sounds fairly all-inclusive. "Continually" doesn't make much allowance for items the Lord doesn't care about.

Elder Bruce R. McConkie taught that the Lord is eager for us to seek, ask, and even weary Him with our petitions. Said he: "*It is pleasing* to that God whose we are *when we fast and pray and seek his blessings;* When we plead with all the energy of our souls for those things we so much desire; When, as Paul says, we 'come boldly unto the throne of grace, that we may obtain mercy, and find grace to help in time of need' (Hebrews 4:16)" (*Ensign,* May 1984, 32; emphasis added).

Elder McConkie also explained that "there is no limit to the revelations each member of the Church may receive. It is within the power of *every person* who has received the gift of the Holy Ghost to see visions, entertain angels, learn the deep and hidden mysteries of the kingdom, and even see the face of God" (*A New Witness for the Articles of Faith,* 490).

Notice his choice of words: *No limit* to revelation. *Every one* of us is eligible. And the privileges are mind-boggling: seeing visions, entertaining angels, learning the hidden mysteries of godliness, and even seeing the face of God.

President Harold B. Lee shared an example from his own life demonstrating just how real communication beyond the veil can be: "I was around ten or eleven years of age," he explained. "I was with my father out on a farm away from our home, trying to spend the day busying myself until my father was ready to go home. Over the fence from our place were some tumbledown sheds that would attract a curious boy, and I was adventurous. I started to climb through the fence, and I heard a voice as clearly as you are hearing mine, calling me by name and saying, 'Don't go over there!' I turned to look at my father to see if he were talking to me, but he was way up at the other end of the field. There was no person in sight. I realized then, as a child, that there were persons beyond my sight, for I had definitely heard a voice. Since then, when I hear or read stories of the Prophet Joseph Smith, I too have known what it means to hear a voice, because I've had the experience" (*Stand Ye in Holy Places*, 139).

Prophets, seers, and revelators throughout our dispensation have confirmed that the Lord's promises about communicating with the heavens truly do apply to all who diligently seek to come out of the world, to come unto the Lord, and to help build the kingdom of God.

Said Brigham Young: "Were I to draw a distinction in *all the duties that are required* of the children of men, from first to last, I would place first and foremost the duty of seeking unto the Lord our God until we open the path of communication from heaven to earth—from God to our own souls.

Keep every avenue of your hearts clean and pure before him" (*Discourses of Brigham Young*, 41; emphasis added).

Again, with reference to the woman who scolded her sister for relying so heavily and so faithfully upon the Lord, consider these words from Elder McConkie: "Is it proper to seek for spiritual gifts? Should we plead with the Lord for the gift of prophecy, or of revelation, or of tongues? Is it fitting and right to pray for the soul-sanctifying privilege of seeing the face of the Lord Jesus while we yet dwell as mortals in a sin-filled world? Does the Lord expect us to desire and seek for spiritual experiences, or do the divine proprieties call for us simply to love the Lord and keep his commandments, knowing that if and when he deems it proper he will grant special gifts and privileges to us?

"By way of answer, it almost suffices to ask such questions as these: Are we not expected to seek salvation, the greatest of all the gifts of God? Why, then, should we not prepare ourselves for this greatest of all boons by seeking the enjoyment of the lesser ones?" (*A New Witness for the Articles of Faith*, 368–69).

In the very first verse of the Book of Mormon, where Nephi essentially set the stage for his record and provided a brief but insightful summary of his life, he acknowledged that while he had seen many afflictions in the course of his day, he had also been "highly favored of the Lord in all [his] days." He then offered his definition of being highly favored—that he had been gifted with "a great knowledge of the goodness and the mysteries of God" (1 Nephi 1:1). If we had nothing other than the first verse of the Book of Mormon, we would know about both the possibility and desirability of learning those things about the kingdom and the workings of God that can be taught only by the Holy Ghost.

For that matter, even Amulek, who became temporarily distracted by the world and its wealth, admitted that the Lord had at least attempted to open up the heavens to him: "I never have known much of the ways of the Lord, and his mysteries and marvelous power," he began, then quickly reversed himself with, "I mistake, for I have seen much of his mysteries and his marvelous power" (Alma 10:5).

In modern revelation, the Lord has declared that there are those who will "have the privilege of receiving the mysteries of the kingdom of heaven," who will "have the heavens opened unto them," who will "commune with the general assembly and church of the Firstborn," and who will "enjoy the communion and presence of God the Father, and Jesus the mediator of the new covenant" (D&C 107:19).

The Lord also explained to the Prophet Joseph that He delights to honor those who serve Him in righteousness and truth to the end by revealing "all mysteries, yea, all the hidden mysteries of my kingdom from days of old, and for ages to come. . . . Yea, even the wonders of eternity shall they know. . . . And their wisdom shall be great, and their understanding reach to heaven. . . . For by my Spirit will I enlighten them, and by my power will I make known unto them the secrets of my will—yea, even those things which eye has not seen, nor ear heard, nor yet entered into the heart of man" (D&C 76:7–10; compare 1 Corinthians 2:9–10).

Unfortunately, perhaps too many of us are content to simply move through our days and weeks, attempting to keep the distractions of the world at bay, even working hard to serve the Lord and fulfill our various obligations. But we don't act as if we believe in the Lord's promises regarding our spiritual privileges. We don't really believe He will tutor us personally regarding the hidden doctrines of the kingdom. We're not riveted on the teachings of prophets, seers, and revelators. We don't dive into the doctrine to gain a sense of the magnitude of what the Lord has promised us. Maybe we're afraid that somehow we're not worthy enough to partake of all our Father and His Son have to offer. And those incorrect beliefs and fears keep us from seeking and studying and laboring diligently to learn and know.

C. S. Lewis believed that "we are half-hearted creatures,

fooling about with drink and sex and ambition when infinite joy is offered us, like an ignorant child who wants to go on making mud pies in a slum because he cannot imagine what is meant by the offer of a holiday at the sea" (*The Weight of Glory and Other Addresses*, 2).

One scriptural passage in the Doctrines and Covenants seems to speak precisely about those of us who are happy making mud pies rather than accepting the offer to vacation at the seashore. Describing those who will not receive a celestial glory, the Lord declared, "They shall return again to their own place, to enjoy that which they are *willing* to receive, because they were *not willing to enjoy that which they might have received*. For what doth it profit a man if a gift is bestowed upon him, and he receive not the gift? Behold, he rejoices not in that which is given unto him, neither rejoices in him who is the giver of the gift" (D&C 88:32–33; emphasis added).

Ugh! It is impossible to imagine or quantify the regret

> *While life is meant to test and challenge and strengthen us, if we are attempting to negotiate the twists and turns and ups and downs of mortality alone, we're doing it all wrong.*

we'll feel if we fail to inherit celestial glory precisely because we weren't willing to—meaning, it's *our* choice. Further, those who don't receive this most transcendent of all gifts will fail to rejoice in the gift itself as well as in the Giver of the gift.

Very simply, signs follow them that believe. Whenever the Lord has His people on the earth, signs attend them. Miracles and gifts of the Spirit attend them. He endows them with power from on high (see D&C 109:22). And He teaches those who are willing and who diligently seek after Him how to draw the powers of heaven into their daily lives.

The bottom line is simple: While life is meant to test and challenge and strengthen us, if we are attempting to negotiate the twists and turns and ups and downs of mortality alone, we're doing it all wrong. Mortality is a test, but it is an open-book test. We have access not only to the divine text but to Him who authored it. But we must approach and seek after Him.

When General George Washington characterized the challenge his ragtag band of colonist soldiers faced during the heat of the Revolutionary War, he essentially described our trial, here in the latter part of the latter days, placed in mortality squarely in the heat of the most intense of all battles between good and evil. Said General Washington: "The fate of unborn millions will now depend, under God, on the courage and conduct of this army" (in David McCullough, *1776*, 13).

Likewise, the fate of the future of the kingdom of God rests in our hands. This Church depends upon a testimony of God the Father, His Son Jesus Christ, and His restored gospel, filling the hearts of millions of men and women, boys and girls, spanning the globe. Thus, the future of the Church depends upon the strength of our testimonies, the strength of our families, the strength of our convictions, and the strength of our willingness to diligently study the gospel and seek after the Lord.

If we're trying to make our way through life on our own, relying largely upon our own talents and strengths and abilities, at some point we will fall short. But if we learn to draw the power of God into our lives, to open our minds to the spiritual privileges and possibilities right in front of us, there is literally no limit to what we may learn and come to understand. There is no limit to the godly power upon which we may learn to draw. There is no limit to the refinement that can and will take place in our natures as we become more and more like our Father and His Son, and no limit to the inheritance we may ultimately receive.

Life is designed to be challenging precisely so that we will turn to our Father, learn about Him and His Son, commit above all else to follow Jesus Christ, and then spend every day of our lives learning more about Him and His gospel—a gospel that is filled with peace and hope and power. Power to rend the heavens and part the veil. Power to overcome evil. Power to turn our mortal frailties and our individual weaknesses into strengths. Power to become, in time, just like Him.

He never intended us to attempt this phase of our eternal existence alone—separated from Him, yes, but never alone. And never alienated or severed from Him. Never!

God is our Father. We were created in His image, and thus our eternal DNA is filled with divinity. Our Father bestows all heavenly and eternal gifts: the gift of charity, the gift of His fulness, the gift of inheriting all that He has and becoming exactly like He is, the gift of perfection, and ultimately the gift of eternal life. Jesus is the Christ, our Redeemer and Savior and King. His Atonement is filled with both redeeming and enabling power. Because He came and did what He was sent to do, because He bore the weight of all the sin and pain of the world, we have access to divine power to help us deal with challenges we could never handle on our own, to find the peace that passeth understanding even in anxious, heartbreaking times.

We worship the Father when we follow His Son. And it is by becoming *true followers* of Jesus Christ that we qualify for the gifts and blessings our Father has for us.

No one loves us more than our Father and the Son. No one understands us better. No one is more eager for us to succeed. And no one better comprehends exactly what we each need to experience in order to return and live with them.

May we therefore devote all our days, all our energy to heeding the word of God and diligently seeking after Him and His Son. For therein lies pure joy.

BOOKS CITED

Barbara Neff Autograph Book. Salt Lake City: Church Historical Department Archives.

Burton, Alma P., ed. *Discourses of the Prophet Joseph Smith.* Salt Lake City: Deseret Book, 1977.

Cannon, George Q. *Gospel Truth: Discourses and Writings of President George Q. Cannon.* Selected, arranged, and edited by Jerreld L. Newquist. Salt Lake City: Deseret Book, 1987.

Dahl, Larry E., and Donald Q. Cannon, eds. *Encyclopedia of Joseph Smith's Teachings.* Salt Lake City: Deseret Book, 2000.

Ehat, Andrew F., and Lyndon W. Cook, eds. *The Words of Joseph Smith: The Contemporary Accounts of the Nauvoo Discourses of the Prophet Joseph.* Second edition, revised. Salt Lake City: Bookcraft, 1996.

Holland, Jeffrey R. *Christ and the New Covenant: The Messianic*

Message of the Book of Mormon. Salt Lake City: Deseret Book, 1997.

Journal of Discourses. 26 vols. London: Latter-day Saints' Book Depot, 1854–1886.

Lee, Harold B. *Stand Ye in Holy Places.* Salt Lake City: Deseret Book, 1975.

Lewis, C. S. *Mere Christianity.* New York: Simon and Schuster, 1996.

———. *The Weight of Glory and Other Addresses.* Grand Rapids, Michigan: William B. Eerdman's Publishing Company, 1965.

Madsen, Carol Cornwall. *In Their Own Words: Women and the Story of Nauvoo.* Salt Lake City: Deseret Book, 1994.

McConkie, Bruce R. *A New Witness for the Articles of Faith.* Salt Lake City: Deseret Book, 1985.

McCullough, David. *1776.* New York: Simon and Schuster, 2005.

Proctor, Maurine Jensen, and Scot Facer Proctor. *The Gathering: Mormon Pioneers on the Trail to Zion.* Salt Lake City: Deseret Book, 1996.

Smith, Joseph, Jr. *History of The Church of Jesus Christ of Latter-day Saints.* 7 vols. Salt Lake City: The Church of Jesus Christ of Latter-day Saints, 1932–1951.

———. *Lectures on Faith.* Salt Lake City: Deseret Book, 1985.

———. *Teachings of the Prophet Joseph Smith.* Joseph Fielding Smith, ed. Salt Lake City: Deseret Book, 1976.

Widtsoe, John A. *Joseph Smith—Seeker after Truth, Prophet of God.* Salt Lake City: Bookcraft, 1951.

Young, Brigham. *Discourses of Brigham Young.* Selected and arranged by John A. Widtsoe. Salt Lake City: Deseret Book, 1954.

INDEX